Cadbury's
CHOCOLATE NOVELTY
— COOKBOOK —

Patricia Dunbar

CHANCELLOR
❦ PRESS ❧

Photography by Mike Vines and Richard London,
The Photographic Studio, Cadbury Schweppes, Bournville, Birmingham
Title spread and pages 55, 63 and 75, by Bob
Challinor of Worcester

The author and publishers would like to thank Kings Norton Cycles,
Cotteridge, Birmingham for kindly supplying the trains shown on
page 38.

Acknowledgement
I owe a very large debt of gratitude to my team of home economists,
both past and present. In particular, I should like to thank Julia
Schofield and Sheelin Robinson for contributing so much and for tirelessly
testing the recipes. Karen has been out in the kitchen too but has
mainly done the typing, with Carole - my thanks to them all.

Previously published in 1989 by
The Hamlyn Publishing Group Limited
part of Reed International Books
under the title Cadbury's Novelty Cakes and Biscuits

This edition published in 1991 by
Chancellor Press
Michelin House, 81 Fulham Road, London SW3 6RB

Reprinted 1992

© Copyright Cadbury Schweppes P.L.C. 1983

ISBN 1 85152 113 5

Filmset in 11 on 12 Bembo by Thameside Filmsetting Ltd,
Ashton-under-Lyne, Lancashire
Line drawings by Roberta Colgate-Stone

Produced by Mandarin Offset
Printed and Bound in China

Cadbury's
CHOCOLATE NOVELTY
— COOKBOOK —

Contents

Using Chocolate Products

The taste of chocolate is universally popular and, to many, quite irresistible. It is therefore easy to understand why some of the most famous specialities of the great chefs of the world are made with chocolate.

There are many varieties of chocolate and cocoa-based products, from dessert chocolate to those that make warming drinks – virtually all are suitable for culinary use. Within this book, Cadbury products have been used in a variety of ways both to make the recipes and to enhance the finished appearance – so important when creating novelty shapes.

Chocolate products fall into several categories. The main ingredients of chocolate are cocoa mass and cocoa butter derived from the cocoa bean, sugar and, in the case of milk chocolate, milk solids. For the best flavour and results, make sure you use true chocolate, not one of the chocolate-flavoured coatings which taste significantly different.

Bournville Dark plain chocolate is a semi-sweet dessert chocolate, particularly suitable for super recipes when the end result and quality of the chocolate flavour is important. The easiest way to melt this chocolate is to place the bar, whole or broken into pieces, into a bowl suspended over a pan of hot, not boiling, water. Turn off the heat and leave the chocolate to melt, without stirring. Avoid letting the chocolate come into contact with water or steam and over-heating, as this could make the chocolate thick and lose its shine. Chocolate stores well in a cool, dark place for up to a year.

Bournville Cocoa is the most economical method of obtaining a good chocolate flavour in cooking. The starch cells in the cocoa need to be broken down so it is therefore better when cocoa is thoroughly cooked, through baking or by blending with a boiling liquid. Always use a dry spoon to measure out the cocoa and close the container after use. Cocoa also keeps for about a year, in a cool dry place.

Drinking Chocolate has a milder flavour and is primarily intended for drinks, as the name implies. It is lighter in colour than cocoa and has added sugar, therefore the sugar quantity in recipes should be adjusted. It is particularly successful in frostings, icings and cakes or biscuits. Bournvita is a malted chocolate drink which gives a characteristic taste to the recipes in which it is used. Chocolate Spread makes an easy cake filling and can also be swirled through a cake mixture.

A crumbled bar of Cadbury's Flake, or coarsely grated chocolate, makes a quick cake decoration as well as being able to be used in more ambitious ways. Milk chocolate Buttons have always been a favourite with young children but have proved to be exceptionally versatile for cake decorations. Creme Eggs and Mini Eggs make any recipe special and are, of course, particularly appropriate around Easter time.

Cadbury's chocolate-covered biscuits are delicious to eat but, once again, are extremely adaptable. Finger biscuits in particular make superb 'fences, roofs or legs', to suggest but a few ideas. Cadbury's Animals, the special children's biscuit, can be quickly stuck on to cakes and the range of round-shaped biscuits such as Cadbury's Shorties, Coasters and the new Chocolate Shortcake, half covered in the distinctive Cadbury's chocolate, all add taste and texture to any recipe in which they are used.

The Developing Art of Entertaining

Throughout history, eating has been a social occasion and 'breaking bread' together a sign of friendship. Sumptuous meals, banquets and feasts, set off by imaginative and eye-catching centrepieces have long been held to celebrate all kinds of important events. The decoration of food to make it look more festive also dates from early times. In ancient Greece, a cook was regarded as an artist who had an important role in society.

The English came to excel in the sweet dishes which formed the dessert course and which were considered to be the most pleasurable part of the meal. English subtleties became renowned all over Europe and were the forerunners of the centrepieces with which the great English and French chefs decorated royal tables in the eighteenth and nineteenth centuries. Elaborate sweet dishes were sculpted or moulded into splendid shapes: lions, birds, crowns, coats of arms; even, as in a feast given by Cardinal Wolsey, the form of a chess board, complete with chessmen.

The cooks were amazingly inventive as it was their chance to please and amaze a great company. They used entirely edible materials – chiefly marchpane, a forerunner of marzipan, stiff fruit pastes and moulded sugar. Later still, chocolate was moulded or carved into wonderous shapes and even today these ingredients are regarded as special.

The Advent of Afternoon Tea

Afternoon tea became popular in Victorian times and this was when the grandest cakes that we know today really developed. The earliest English cakes were spiced and sweetened breads but they soon became more extravagant with icing and decorations. Traditional English rich fruit cakes were developed and became renowned throughout the world and are the basis of many celebration cakes. Birthday cakes, christening cakes, wedding cakes, Christmas cakes and a simnel cake at Easter are still popular. Every country seems to have its own festive specialities – the Christmas gingerbread house in Germany, Russian Mazurka cake or Polish Easter ring are examples.

Celebrations Today

Much of today's food appears quite frugal in comparison with the ostentation of our forefathers. Nevertheless, we still prepare grand meals when the occasion demands and very often the centrepiece is a cake or gâteau. This may be lovingly prepared for another member of the family or for a friend or a special celebration. Today, many people may only bake a special cake four or five times a year. All the more reason for it to be a really super one!

Entertaining with Ease

Some people seem to be natural party givers, able to cope with large numbers of guests on any occasion with seemingly minimum fuss. Others approach the prospect of social occasions, such as children's birthday parties, an inescapable event in every child's calendar, with fear and trepidation.

For both categories, forward planning and a little common sense will help to make all social occasions enjoyable to both guests and hosts. So here are some hints for a successful party whatever the occasion.

● Plan well in advance – the type of party, number of guests, theme (if applicable), food to be served and entertainment to be organised. Try to make as many things as possible in advance. If you have a food freezer, make it work for you.

● As a guide to amounts for a *children's party*, allow 4 – 6 savoury items (including crisps, cheese snacks or sausages), 2 sweet items, ice-cream and jelly, birthday cake and 2 cold drinks. An 850 ml bottle of Schweppes fruit squash will give 20 – 24 servings when diluted.

● For an adult tea party, allow 3 – 4 savoury items, 2 small cakes, 1 slice of a special cake and 2 cups of tea. When large numbers are to be catered for, allow a minimum of 35 g/ $1\frac{1}{2}$ oz of Typhoo tea to a gallon of boiling water.

● Try not to be over-ambitious. Remember the limitations of house size or garden and your culinary ability.

● Send invitations out in plenty of time. Two or three weeks' notice is generally accepted but for formal occasions like weddings, six weeks should be allowed.

● Sort out cutlery, china and glasses the day before. For large parties, it is often a good idea to hire china and glasses. Use paper plates for informal or children's parties. Set the table the night before or designate another member of the family to do it on the day.

● Finally, allow yourself time to relax and change in peace before the guests arrive. You will enjoy the party much more.

Giving a children's party can be the most rewarding form of entertainment but takes a little more effort to organise successfully. One of the high spots of the party is undoubtedly the birthday cake although they are not always actually eaten!

There are lots of ideas in this book to bring cries of delight from all ages.

Fun invitations with matching plates, paper cups and napkins are easily available but why not make the cards yourself, or get older children to help? All that is needed is a template of the design – a teddy bear for a teddy bear's picnic or a zoo animal for an outing to the zoo are examples. Writing the message on a balloon can also be fun. Balloons are a must for games or take-home presents. Children also love streamers and blowers. The cake centrepiece should preferably fit into the chosen theme – such as the Country Cake, with each child being given a toy farm animal as a small present.

Party Games

Every family has its favourite party game and young guests come to expect it in the programme. Blend noisy and quiet games and remember to allow time for free expression – or 'fighting' time as many young boys seem to want! Eight-year olds and above seem to like educational games such as Kim's game, match stick problems, making words or odd man out.

Here are just some of my particular favourites to start you thinking.

Down on the Farm (for younger children)
Evolve a story about a farm (or zoo) mentioning the various animals. The children make the animal noises and on occasions, imitate the actions, amid shrieks of laughter.

Pass the Parcel
Wrap a small present in the centre of a large parcel with many layers of paper. Include a few sweets between the layers. Lots of mess whilst it's being undone but the children do sit down!

Scissors (older children and adults)
A game of observation, handing the scissors round a circle of people and announcing 'crossed' or 'uncrossed' as they are passed. In fact, it is not the scissors you are referring to but your legs!

Team Games
Old favourites include spoon ball (passing a ping pong ball along a line, balanced in teaspoons held in the mouth), passing oranges under the chin, blowing ping pong balls with drinking straws and fanning the kipper.

Useful Facts and Figures

Oven temperatures

The table below gives recommended equivalents.

	°C	°F	Gas Mark
Very cool	110	225	$\frac{1}{4}$
	120	250	$\frac{1}{2}$
Cool or Slow	140	275	1
	150	300	2
Warm	160	325	3
Moderate	180	350	4
Moderately hot	190	375	5
Fairly hot	200	400	6
Hot	220	425	7
Very hot	230	450	8
	240	475	9

Notes for American and Australian users

In America the 8-oz measuring cup is used. In Australia metric measures are now used in conjunction with the standard 250-ml measuring cup. The imperial pint, used in Britain and Australia, is 20 fl oz, while the American pint is 16 fl oz. It is important to remember that the Australian tablespoon differs from both the British and American tablespoons; the table below gives a comparison. The British standard tablespoon, which has been used throughout this book, holds 17.7 ml, the American 14.2 ml, and the Australian 20 ml. A teaspoon holds approximately 5 ml in all three countries.

British	American	Australian
1 teaspoon	1 teaspoon	1 teaspoon
1 tablespoon	1 tablespoon	1 tablespoon
2 tablespoons	3 tablespoons	2 tablespoons
$3\frac{1}{2}$ tablespoons	4 tablespoons	3 tablespoons
4 tablespoons	5 tablespoons	$3\frac{1}{2}$ tablespoons

Spoon measures All spoon measures given in this book are level unless otherwise stated.

❄ Denotes freezing instructions.
Denotes helpful hint.

An Imperial/American guide to solid and liquid measures

Imperial	American
Solid measures	
1 lb butter or margarine	2 cups
1 lb flour	4 cups
1 lb granulated or caster sugar	2 cups
1 lb icing sugar	3 cups
Liquid measures	
$\frac{1}{4}$ pint liquid	$\frac{2}{3}$ cup liquid
$\frac{1}{2}$ pint	$1\frac{1}{4}$ cups
$\frac{3}{4}$ pint	2 cups
1 pint	$2\frac{1}{2}$ cups
$1\frac{1}{2}$ pints	$3\frac{3}{4}$ cups
2 pints	5 cups ($2\frac{1}{2}$ pints)

Useful baking tin comparisons

There are many occasions when the exact sized baking tin may not be available or when you wish to make a particular cake recipe in another shape. The following conversions might prove useful.
800-ml/$1\frac{1}{2}$-pint pudding basin =
    14-cm/$5\frac{1}{2}$-in round deep cake tin
1.2-litre/2-pint pudding basin =
    15-cm/6-in round deep cake tin or 12.5-cm/5-in square deep tin

Loaf tins

1-kg/2-lb loaf tin =
    28 × 18-cm/11 × 7-in shallow tin
0.5-kg/1-lb loaf tin =
    18-cm/7-in square shallow cake tin or a
    33 × 23-cm/13 × 9-in Swiss roll tin
The capacity of a round tin is equal to that of a square cake tin which is 2.5 cm/1 in smaller in size, for example a 20-cm/8-in round tin holds the same quantity as an 18-cm/7-in square tin. This can be adjusted to the nearest 1.25 cm/$\frac{1}{2}$ in.

Cooking times given in the recipe will have to be adjusted to suit the new tin size.

NOTE: When making any of the recipes in this book, only follow one set of measures as they are not interchangeable

First Things First

No matter how complicated a decoration, the cake underneath tastes just as appetising as it looks. In this chapter are the basic cake and icing recipes which are used for many of the novelties in this book. You will also find clear instructions for lining cake tins and making piping bags – all the information you need for completing the design.

Chocolate Victoria Sponge Cake

(Illustrated on page 6)

Metric		Imperial
175 g	margarine	6 oz
175 g	caster or soft brown sugar	6 oz
3	eggs, size 2 or 3	3
150 g	self-raising flour	5 oz
25 g	Bournville Cocoa	1 oz
	Filling	
350 g	chocolate butter icing (page 16)	12 oz
2 (19-cm)	round shallow cake tins	2 (7½-in)
	greaseproof paper	

Prepare the cake tins by cutting out two circles of greaseproof paper the same size as the base of the tins. Grease the tins, put the paper circles in them and also grease the paper.

Cream the margarine and sugar together really well until pale and soft; an electric mixer is ideal for this. Add the eggs one at a time, with a spoonful of flour if the mixture shows any signs of curdling. Sift the flour and cocoa together and fold in, adding a little milk or orange juice if the mixture is too dry, as it should have a soft dropping consistency. Divide the mixture in spoonfuls evenly between the tins, then spread the surface flat and hollow out the centres slightly. Bake in the centre of a moderately hot oven (190 C, 375 F, gas 5) for about 30 minutes until risen and springy to the touch. Leave the cakes in the tin for a moment before turning out on to a wire tray. Peel off the greaseproof paper and immediately turn the cakes over again to avoid any marks on the top. Leave to cool.

Sandwich the cakes together with half the butter icing and spread the remainder on top. Mark with a fork.

Wrap and freeze the cake complete or place greaseproof paper in between the cake layers and freeze them separately.

A 2-egg quantity of the cake mixture can be made in two 15–18-cm/6–7-in sandwich tins. If preferred, plain flour can be used instead of self-raising flour, allowing 5 ml/ 1 teaspoon of baking powder to every 50 g/2 oz of the flour and cocoa weighed together.

The cake mixture can also be cooked in a deep cake tin but increase the baking time to about 55 minutes. Cover with a piece of paper if the cake becomes too crisp on top during cooking. Stand deep and loose-based tins on baking trays.

Plain Victoria sponge cake
To make a plain Victoria sponge cake, omit the cocoa from the above recipe and use 175 g/6 oz self-raising flour. Continue according to the instructions.

Cutting circles of grease-proof paper for sandwich tins *It is useful to have a store of greaseproof paper circles ready cut out for instant use.*

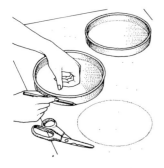

To vary the quantity The recipes require different quantities of this mixture, for example the ingredients may refer to a '6 egg quantity'. The recipe given is a 3 egg quantity and can be adjusted by reducing or increasing the ingredients in proportion to the number of eggs.

One Stage Method

Use soft margarine. Mix all the ingredients together in a bowl; 5 ml/1 teaspoon baking powder may also be added to the cake ingredients. Beat really hard for 2–3 minutes until completely blended. Bake the cakes as usual.

Pudding Basin Cake

(Illustrated on page 6)

Lining a deep cake tin

1 *Cut a piece of greaseproof paper to fit the base. Cut a strip of paper, deeper than the sides of the tin and long enough to go all around the inside. Make regular snips about 1 cm/¼ in deep along the strip of paper.*

2 *Grease the tin and ease the strip of paper in around the side, overlapping the snipped edge in the base. Lay the piece neatly in the base of the tin and grease thoroughly.*

Metric		Imperial
175 g	butter or margarine	6 oz
175 g	caster sugar	6 oz
3	eggs, size 3	3
150 g	self-raising flour	5 oz
5 ml	baking powder	1 teaspoon
25 g	Bournville Cocoa	1 oz
1	small orange	1
	orange food colouring	
1.2-litre	ovenproof basin, greased	2-pint
	baking tray	

Cream the fat and sugar until light in colour and texture. Gradually add the eggs, then fold in the flour and baking powder sifted together. In a separate mixing bowl, blend the cocoa to a paste with a little boiling water, then add half the cake mixture to it and mix well. Finely grate the orange rind and add it to the remaining mixture with enough strained orange juice to make a soft dropping consistency. Add colouring if liked. Spoon the two mixtures alternately into the basin then swirl through *only once* so that they remain separate. Smooth the top and hollow out the centre slightly. Stand the cake on a baking tray and cook in a moderate oven (180 C, 350 F, gas 4) for 1–1¼ hours until cooked through. When cooked, a warm skewer inserted into the middle of the cake should come out cleanly. Turn out and cool on a wire tray.

Use the cake as required in a variety of recipes.

Chocolate Swiss Roll

(Illustrated on page 6)

Metric		Imperial
3	**fresh eggs, size 2**	3
75 g	**caster sugar**	3 oz
	vanilla essence	
75 g	**plain flour**	3 oz
25 g	**Bournville Cocoa**	1 oz
20 ml	**warm water**	1 tablespoon
	Filling	
175 g	**plain butter icing (page 16) or**	6 oz
142 ml	**whipping cream**	$\frac{1}{4}$ pint
23 × 33-cm	**Swiss roll tin, greased and lined**	9 × 13-in
	greaseproof paper	

Freezes well.

This type of sponge depends on the air being whisked in for its success. When the mixture is stiff enough, you should be able to write three initials in it without them disappearing immediately. If in doubt, continue whisking for a few more minutes. If you are repeatedly unsuccessful with this technique, try adding 5 ml/1 teaspoon baking powder with the flour.

Whisk the eggs, sugar and a few drops of essence in a bowl over a pan of hot water, or use an electric mixer. Whisk hard until the mixture is thick enough to leave a definite trail from the whisk. Sift the flour and cocoa together then fold in with a metal spoon, adding the water at the same time. Ensure there are no pockets of flour left. Turn the mixture into the prepared tin and tilt the tin to level the mixture – on no account spread it. Bake in a pre-set, fairly hot oven (200 C, 400 F, gas 6) for about 12 minutes until cooked when the sponge will be risen and springy to the touch.

Dust a large piece of greaseproof paper with caster sugar. Carefully turn the Swiss roll out on to this and gently peel off the paper. With a large sharp knife, trim off the crisp edges. Mark a dent along one short side about 1 cm/$\frac{1}{2}$ in from the edge. Lay another piece of greaseproof paper on top and roll the cake up, with the paper inside. Leave on a wire tray to cool.

Carefully unroll the Swiss roll and take off the paper. Spread with butter icing or whipped cream, taking it right up to the edges. Starting with the marked end, roll up as tightly as possible without squashing the cake. Dust with sugar: icing, caster or even soft brown sugar for example. *Serves 6*

Plain Swiss roll To make a plain Swiss roll, omit the cocoa and continue as above. Spread jam over the freshly cooked sponge and roll up as described.

To line a Swiss roll tin

1 *Cut out a rectangle of greased paper bigger than the tin itself. Grease the tin.*

2 *Lay the paper in the tin, pressing it right into the corners. Make a cut down into the corners of the paper and fold the edges behind each other to make a neat corner. Also grease the paper.*

Fairy Castle (page 65) and Anniversary Cake (page 60)

Chocolate Buns

Metric		Imperial
	2 egg quantity	
	chocolate Victoria sponge cake (page 12)	
15–20	**paper cake cases**	15–20
	bun tins or baking tray	

Make up the cake mixture, by the one-stage method if preferred. Place the paper cases in the bun tins or close together on a baking tray and put a good teaspoonful of cake mixture into each. Bake in a moderately hot oven (190 C, 375 F, gas 5) for about 15 minutes until the buns are risen and spring back when touched. *Makes 15–20*

Dariole cakes The above mixture can be cooked in 12–15 dariole (castle pudding) tins, depending on their capacity. Cook the cakes in a moderately hot oven (190 C, 375 F, gas 5) for about 20 minutes.

This recipe can be made using a 3 egg quantity in which case it will make 25–30 buns. Do not be tempted to fill the paper cases too full if the buns are to be iced.

Additional flavourings are easy to add for variety. For example, try the *Frosty Bear* cheese cake mixture (page 110).

Chocolate Butter Icing

Metric		Imperial
25 g	**Bournville Cocoa**	1 oz
60 ml	**boiling water**	3 tablespoons
175 g	**butter or soft margarine**	6 oz
250–350 g	**icing sugar, sifted**	9–12 oz
	flavouring (optional)	

Dissolve the cocoa in the boiling water, making a paste. Cream the fat to soften it, then add the icing sugar and beat really well until the mixture becomes pale in colour and light in texture. (An electric mixer is helpful.) Mix in the cooled cocoa.

Additional flavouring of vanilla or peppermint essence, dissolved instant coffee or the finely grated rind of half an orange may be added.

Store in a covered container in the refrigerator or freezer. The quantity of butter icing given in the recipes refers to the weight of butter and sugar added together.

This recipe makes enough butter icing to fill and decorate a 20-cm/8-in sponge cake.

Plain butter icing Omit the Bournville Cocoa but make as above, adding a few drops of vanilla essence.

Add grated lemon rind and a little juice instead of the vanilla essence to make lemon butter icing.

Lining a loaf tin

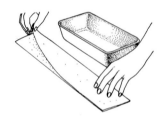

1 Cut a double strip of paper wide enough and long enough to fit along the length of the tin and over both ends.

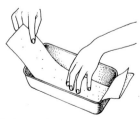

2 Grease the tin and press the paper neatly into it. Grease the paper.

To make a greaseproof paper piping bag

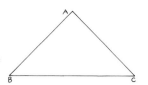

1 *Cut a square of greaseproof paper at least 25 cm/10 in. in diameter, fold in half diagonally, forming a triangle. Make a small slit in the centre of the folded line to help give a sharper point.*

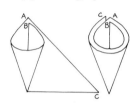

2 *Take corner (B) and roll it so that it lies inside the corner (A).*
3 *Bring corner (C) round the outside of the bag so that it lies exactly behind (A).*

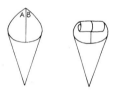

4 *Adjust paper so that all corners are together and there is a sharp tip to the bag.*
5 *Fold over point (A) two or three times to keep bag together.*
6 *If an icing pipe is used, snip a small piece off the point and drop in selected pipe. To use the bag on its own, fill with icing then cut off tip.*

Glacé Icing

Metric		Imperial
225 g	**icing sugar, sifted**	8 oz
about 40 ml	**warm water or fruit juice**	about 2 tablespoons
	food colouring	

Stir the icing sugar with the water or preferably fruit juice, in a bowl, adding colouring if needed. Mix until absolutely smooth and use immediately as a skin quickly forms on the surface.

This amount is enough to coat the top of a popular sized (15–20-cm/6–8-in) sponge.

Royal Icing

Metric		Imperial
225 g	**icing sugar, sifted**	8 oz
1	**egg white, size 2**	1
5 ml	**glycerine**	1 teaspoon
5 ml	**lemon juice, strained**	1 teaspoon

Beat all the ingredients together, preferably with an electric mixer, until the icing is absolutely white and standing in peaks. The longer it is beaten, the better the icing will be. Always keep prepared icing covered until it is used.

Cup Cake Icing

Metric		Imperial
50 g	**butter**	2 oz
60 ml	**water**	3 tablespoons
225 g	**icing sugar**	8 oz
50 g	**Bournville Cocoa**	2 oz

Melt the butter and water in a saucepan. Take off the heat before sifting in the icing sugar and cocoa. Beat until smooth and glossy. Use the icing warm to coat a batch of small cakes.

This quantity will coat 25–30 small cakes.

Simply Appealing

Here is a selection of cakes which are easy to decorate and quite irresistible. Whatever the occasion, there is something for everyone – a Sweetheart Surprise, perhaps, or Pretty Maid for the older members of the family or for the younger ones, the White Rabbit or Frogland. Each design has a distinct character of its own which is, indeed, simply appealing.

Mushroom Cakes

(Illustrated opposite)

Pack the mushroom cakes carefully and freeze complete.

Choose a tray of fairly shallow, *plain* patty tins. The fluted or decorative tins are not suitable as they do not look like mushrooms when turned out, and the marzipan is more likely to stick to the tins.

Metric		Imperial
225 g	marzipan	8 oz
	a little icing sugar, sifted	
75 g	butter	3 oz
100 g	Bournville Dark plain chocolate	3½ oz
125 g	desiccated coconut	4 oz
50 g	glacé cherries, chopped	2 oz
50 g	sweet biscuits, crushed	2 oz
20 ml	brandy or fruit juice	1 tablespoon
6	Cadbury's Flake from the Family Pack	6
	a little Cadbury's Drinking Chocolate	
7-cm	plain cutter	2½-in
	12 patty tins	

Roll out the marzipan on a surface lightly dusted with icing sugar. Using the biscuit cutter, cut out twelve circles, re-rolling the trimmings in between. Line the patty tins with the marzipan, rather like pastry tarts. Melt the butter with the broken up chocolate, coconut, chopped cherries and crushed biscuits in a saucepan, heating gently and stirring frequently. Stir in the brandy or fruit juice and mix well before dividing this mixture between the marzipan cases. Fork over the top of the mixture, towards the centre then leave to cool.

Cut the Flakes in half and stand a piece in the centre of each mushroom cake, pushing it in gently but firmly. Leave the mixture to set completely before removing from the tins with a palette knife. Be careful not to mark the marzipan. Dust the marzipan with a little sifted drinking chocolate. *Makes 12*

Mushroom Manor (page 56) and Mushroom Cakes

Clarence Caterpillar

(Illustrated on page 75)

Metric		Imperial
1	**chocolate Swiss roll (page 14)**	1
1	**plain Swiss roll (page 14)**	1
25 g	**Bournville Cocoa**	1 oz
350 g	**plain butter icing (page 16)**	12 oz
	green food colouring	
80 ml	**desiccated coconut**	4 tablespoons
2	**Cadbury's Buttons**	2
1	**silver doily**	1
2	**glacé cherries**	2
2	**wooden cocktail sticks**	2
1 packet	**Cadbury's Fingers**	1 packet

62-cm (approximately)	**long board**	15-in (approximately)

The cake freezes well and can be covered with icing but it is best assembled just when it is required. The biscuits do not need freezing.

Cut a slice off each Swiss roll, then cut the two large pieces in half lengthways. Blend the cocoa into a paste with a little boiling water and mix into half the butter icing. Colour the other half green.

Use a little icing to sandwich a chocolate and a jam piece of Swiss roll back together again. Lay the two rolls end to end on the board. Spread alternate broad stripes of chocolate and green icing along the length, covering the rolls completely. Sandwich the two reserved slices of Swiss roll together, then arrange this 'head' at an angle on one end of the roll, pressing it on firmly. Sprinkle the body with coconut. Put a small dot of icing in the centre of each Button and stick both on the front of the head. Curl the doily into a cone shape; trim the edge if it is too large but allow enough for a big, turned-back brim. Stick a cherry on the end of each cocktail stick; place the doily hat in position and press the sticks through the paper into the cake. Finally, halve all the biscuits, cut off one small piece and press it into the head to make a nose. Stick all the rest of the halved biscuits into the base for legs.

Frogland

(Illustrated on page 111)

Depending on the size of the bowl or the number of children to feed, double the amount of jelly and increase the frogs and marshmallow flowers so that there is one of each for each person.

Metric		Imperial
1	**lime flavour jelly**	1
	blue food colouring	
125 g	**plain butter icing (page 16)**	4 oz
10 ml	**Bournville Cocoa**	2 teaspoons
	yellow food colouring	
1 packet	**Cadbury's Buttons**	1 packet
5	**Cadbury's Creme Eggs**	5
5	**glacé cherries**	5
1	**chocolate bun (page 16)**	1
5 or 6	**marshmallows**	5 or 6
14 g	**angelica**	$\frac{1}{2}$ oz
	large shallow glass bowl	
2	**star pipes**	2
2 or 3	**greaseproof paper piping bags**	2 or 3

Make up the jelly as directed on the packet, using slightly less water to give a firm set. Add a little blue food colouring to represent a pond colour, then pour the jelly into the bowl and leave to set.

Have the butter icing ready. Blend the cocoa with enough boiling water to make a thick paste and cool before mixing into one-third of the butter icing. Add yellow food colouring to the remaining amount, making some darker if liked. Cut the tips off the piping bags, drop in the pipes and fill with the different coloured icings. Pipe a chocolate star on ten Buttons, arrange them next to each other in pairs with the butter icing on top, then stand a Creme Egg on top. Complete each 'frog' by piping a line of pale butter icing at one end for the mouth and placing two cherry halves, secured with a little butter icing, above for the protruding eyes. Arrange the frogs on the set jelly, standing one on the cake.

Snip the marshmallows into flowers and pipe a star in the centre of each. Stick them on to the jelly with butter icing and arrange in clusters. Decorate with angelica diamonds and longer pieces of angelica to represent reeds sticking out of the jelly. Additional stars of butter icing and halved Buttons may be put round the edge of the jelly. *Serves 5*

Fantail Chicken

(Illustrated opposite)

Metric		Imperial
3	**eggs, size 2**	3
75 g	**caster sugar**	3 oz
75 g	**plain flour**	3 oz
40 ml	**Bournville Cocoa**	2 tablespoons
5 ml	**baking powder**	1 teaspoon
	Decoration	
450 g	**plain butter icing (page 16)**	1 lb
40 ml	**Bournville Cocoa**	2 tablespoons
1 packet	**Cadbury's Buttons**	1 packet
2 (20-g) bars	**Cadbury's Dairy Milk**	2 small bars
	Chocolate	
4	**glacé cherries**	4
2 (18-cm)	**round shallow cake tins,**	2 (7-in)
	greased and base lined	
	star pipe	
1	**greaseproof paper piping bag**	1

Freeze complete or to save freezer space, finish off the decoration on the thawed cake.

A whisked sponge depends on the air that is whisked into it for a successful rise. If in doubt, whisk the mixture for another 5 minutes; it will not harm the cake.

Birthday candles and holders, particularly red ones, look effective arranged in a curve among the Button tail feathers.

Whisk the eggs and sugar together with an electric mixer, or stand the bowl over a pan of hot water and whisk by hand. Whisk hard until a good trail is visible from the whisk. Sift all the dry ingredients together, then lightly fold into the mixture, ensuring that no pockets of flour remain. Pour into the prepared tins and tip them to level the surface – do not spread the mixture. Bake in a fairly hot oven (200 c, 400 f, gas 6) for about 12 minutes until the cakes are springy and cooked. Cool on a wire tray and peel the paper.

Make up the butter icing. Dissolve the cocoa in a little boiling water then blend into half the icing. Sandwich the cakes together with a layer of chocolate butter icing, then cut in half. Cover one half completely with the plain icing, reserving a little for decoration, and the other half with chocolate icing. Mark the top and sides of both halves with a fork. On a large board or tray perhaps, arrange the two pieces of cake touching in the middle and protruding at either end, as shown in the picture. Fit the star pipe into the piping bag. Place the reserved plain butter icing into the bag, then pipe an eye and a small patch for the wing. Stand the lightly polished Buttons upright in the plain cake tail piece. Cut one bar of chocolate into two triangles and position as the long legs at the base of the cake. Make four triangles from the other bar of chocolate and use two as the beak and two for wings. Cut a serrated edge on the cherries and pile them up near the eye as the cock's comb.

Harriet Hedgehog (page 49), Fantail Chicken and Sausage Dogs (page 109)

Sweetheart Surprise

(Illustrated on page 63)

Metric		Imperial
175 g	**caster sugar**	6 oz
125 ml	**bland vegetable oil**	$\frac{1}{4}$ pint
150 g	**natural yogurt**	5 oz
80 ml	**golden syrup**	4 tablespoons
3	**eggs, size 2**	3
a few drops	**almond essence**	a few drops
225 g	**self-raising flour**	8 oz
90 ml	**Bournville Cocoa**	3 rounded tablespoons
2.5 ml	**bicarbonate of soda**	$\frac{1}{2}$ teaspoon
2.5 ml	**salt**	$\frac{1}{2}$ teaspoon
	Frosting and decoration	
350 g	**apricot jam**	12 oz
175 g	**caster sugar**	6 oz
2	**egg whites**	2
1.25 ml	**cream of tartar**	$\frac{1}{4}$ teaspoon
40 ml	**water**	2 tablespoons
	pink food colouring	
4	**glacé cherries**	4
	angelica	
18-cm	**round deep cake tin, greased and base lined**	7-in
18-cm	**square deep cake tin, greased and base lined**	7-in
30-cm	**heart-shaped or round cake board**	12-in

Beat the sugar, oil, yogurt, syrup, eggs and almond essence together in a large bowl, preferably with an electric mixer, until pale in colour. Sift the dry ingredients together, then fold them into the mixture, making sure no lumps of flour remain. Divide the mixture *equally* between the two prepared tins and bake the cakes in a warm oven (160 C, 325 F, gas 3) for 70–80 minutes until risen, springy to the touch and cooked. Turn out both cakes and cool on a wire tray.

Slice both cakes in half and sandwich them back together with jam. Cut the round cake in half. Assemble the cakes on the board: place the two semi-circles on two sides of the square cake as shown in the diagram. Stick them together with a little jam.

To make the frosting, mix the sugar, egg whites, cream of tartar and water in a large bowl. Stand the bowl over a pan of simmering water, then whisk hard for at least 8 minutes until the frosting thickens, forms soft peaks and becomes really shiny. About half way through, slowly add a few drops of

Freeze the complete cake without covering and when hard, wrap loosely in foil and label. Be careful the icing is not knocked off in the freezer. Alternatively, freeze the cakes alone and decorate them later.

Fold the flour in with a large metal spoon or spatula to ensure the air is not knocked out and that all the flour gets mixed in from the bottom of the bowl. A flat cake generally means too vigorous mixing at this stage. Make sure that the cakes are the same depth in the tin before baking.

An electric hand mixer is best for making this icing as it really needs to be whisked hard. As the frosting thickens, it becomes harder to work but it is essential to make it thick enough or it will not harden on the cake. About 8–10 minutes with an electric mixer is generally enough, but keep the bowl standing over hot water.

Paper doilies make an attractive edge for this cake. Before the cake is assembled secure the doilies in the centre of the board with sticky tape.

Cutting and assembling the cakes

colouring. When the right texture is reached, quickly spread the frosting all over the cake, including the sides, swirling it into soft peaks. Cut three of the cherries into long pieces and cut the last one in half. Arrange a simple flower design on the cake, as shown in the picture, with stalks and leaves of angelica. Leave the icing to harden on the surface, although the underneath remains moist. *Serves 12–16*

Flower Tubs

(Illustrated on page 54)

The easiest way to cut marshmallows is to use scissors which are first dipped in warm water.

Other decorations can be used with the marshmallows: Cadbury's Buttons, sugar strands or coloured small sweets look nice.

Metric		Imperial
100 g	**Bournville Dark plain chocolate**	3½ oz
125 g	**margarine**	4 oz
125 g	**caster sugar**	4 oz
2	**eggs**	2
175 g	**self-raising flour, sifted**	6 oz
80 ml	**concentrated orange squash**	4 tablespoons
	Decoration	
175 g	**chocolate butter icing (page 16)**	6 oz
1 packet	**marshmallows**	1 packet
20	**mimosa sugar balls**	20
20	**paper cake cases**	20
	baking tray	

Chop the chocolate into small pieces. Cream the margarine and sugar well together. Stir in the eggs, then the flour, chocolate and orange squash to make a dropping consistency. Divide the mixture between the cake cases and bake them on the tray in a moderately hot oven (190 c, 375 f, gas 5) for 12–15 minutes until lightly browned, well risen and cooked. Cool on a wire tray.

Prepare the butter icing and spread it neatly on top of the cakes. Slice each marshmallow horizontally into three circles. Pinch one end to elongate each piece into the shape of a petal. Arrange the petals on top of the cakes, with a mimosa ball in the centre of each. *Makes 20*

Rock Garden

(Illustrated opposite)

Metric		Imperial
1 packet	**Cadbury's Shorties**	1 packet
50 g	**butter**	2 oz
1	**egg**	1
25 g	**demerara sugar**	1 oz
125 g	**stoned dates**	4 oz
50 g	**walnut pieces**	2 oz
50 g	**crystallised ginger**	2 oz
	For the flowers	
350 g	**plain butter icing (page 16)**	12 oz
	food colourings	
225 g	**marzipan**	8 oz
about 6	**chocolate buns and dariole**	about 6
	cakes (page 16)	
1 packet	**marshmallows**	1 packet
	a few cherries, sugar balls and angelica	
19-cm	**non-stick flan tin, well greased**	7½-in
	and the centre lined with waxed paper	
	star pipe	
	several greaseproof paper piping bags	

This is an idea where you can really use your imagination. All that is necessary is the basic flan mixture on which to build the 'garden', and a few small chocolate cakes. Use ingredients at hand to make a colourful display. You are sure to have as much fun creating the garden as you will showing it off at the table.

Break up the biscuits quite roughly. Melt the butter, then cool a little before beating in the egg and the sugar. Chop the dates, walnuts and ginger then stir into the butter mixture with the biscuits, mixing really well so that everything is shiny and coated. Press firmly into the prepared flan tin and leave in the refrigerator overnight to firm up. Dip the base of the flan tin into hot water for 5 seconds then tap the mixture out on to a plate. Peel off the paper.

Divide the butter icing into two or three portions and colour each with a different food colour. Similarly, divide and colour the marzipan. Have a few small cakes ready. Roll out the marzipan and cut out 2.5-cm/1-in circles. These are arranged either round the edge of the cakes or on top, pinched in at one end to represent petals. Pipe butter icing to complete the flowers. The tall flowers are butter icing piped on the dariole cakes with a Cadbury's Finger biscuit or Flake base.

To make the marshmallow flowers, cut down into the marshmallows almost through to the base and into six wedges. Pipe a star of butter icing in the centre. Arrange the larger flower cakes on the biscuit flan and fill in the gaps with the smaller sweets, flowers, an assortment of cake decorations, Cadbury's Buttons, cherries and angelica as shown in the picture. *Serves about 8*

Butterfly Cake (page 72), Fingers Cottage (page 64) and Rock Garden

Dominoes

(Illustrated on title spread and page 50)

Metric		Imperial
50 g	**butter**	2 oz
40 ml	**golden syrup**	2 good tablespoons
75 g	**Cadbury's Drinking Chocolate**	3 oz
100 g	**'Rice Krispies'**	3½ oz
40 ml	**royal icing or plain butter icing (pages 17 and 16)**	2 tablespoons
30 × 20-cm	**Swiss roll tin, greased**	12 × 8-in
1	**greaseproof paper piping bag**	1

It is worth using a ruler to make the pieces as even in size as possible. It will be necessary to make double quantities of the recipe if a fun game of dominoes is to be played at the tea table.

Melt the butter and syrup in a saucepan. Remove the pan from the heat and stir in the drinking chocolate and rice krispies, mixing thoroughly until completely coated. Press this mixture firmly into the tin, without breaking up the krispies, and leave to harden.

Cut the mixture in half lengthways, then cut each strip into nine even-sized finger-shaped pieces. Put the icing into the piping bag and cut off the tip. Pipe a line and the required number of dots across each domino, remembering to include a double six or the game cannot start! *Makes 18*

Pirates' Puddings

(Illustrated on title spread and page 78)

Metric		Imperial
50 g	**sponge cake**	2 oz
1 (411-g)	**can fruit cocktail**	1 (14½-oz)
1	**strawberry flavour jelly**	1
1 (150-g)	**carton strawberry yogurt**	1 (5-oz)
50 g	**Bournville Dark plain chocolate, grated**	2 oz
16	**seedless raisins**	16
8	**small walnut pieces**	8
3	**glacé cherries, sliced**	3
8	**ring biscuits from Cadbury's Bournville Assorted**	8
8	**waxed paper trifle cases**	8

If it is easier, the jelly can be left in a cold place until almost set before pouring over the cake and fruit, in which case it can all be added at once. These novel trifles are popular with younger children who like the tanginess of the jelly.

Divide the cake between the trifle cases. Drain the fruit, reserving the syrup to make up the jelly. Add enough water to the syrup to give just over 275 ml/½ pint. Pour this liquid into a saucepan. Add the broken up jelly tablet and stir over low heat until dissolved. Do not allow the jelly to boil. Remove from the heat and allow to cool. Whisk in the yogurt. Spoon the fruit over the cake and pour half the jelly on top. Leave in the refrigerator to thicken so that the fruit does not rise, but do not put the reserved jelly in the refrigerator. Later, pour the remaining jelly on top and leave to set completely.

Sprinkle the chocolate on for hair, arrange raisins as eyes, a piece of walnut for a nose and a slice of cherry for a mouth. Cut the biscuits in half and stick in on either side of the faces. Make them all in the same way. Chill the puddings until ready to eat. *Makes 8*

Sunbathing Penguins

(Illustrated on page 111)

Metric		Imperial
6	**bananas**	6
6	**Cadbury's Flake from the Family Pack**	6
25 g	**chopped nuts**	1 oz
2	**small egg whites**	2
100 g	**caster sugar**	$3\frac{1}{2}$ oz
	baking tray	
	nylon piping bag	
	medium star pipe	

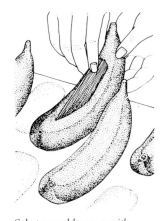

Select curved bananas with pointed stalk ends, to represent beaks. A tray of éclair tins, if available, are ideal to stand the bananas on to keep them upright. Crumpled foil can also be used to support the bananas.

Stand the bananas on the baking tray so that they curve upwards. Bake in a moderate oven (180 c, 350 f, gas 4) for 20–30 minutes until the bananas are black. Make a slit in the skin along the top edge of each banana then push in a Flake. Sprinkle over the nuts. Whisk the egg whites stiffly, add half the sugar and whisk again until just as stiff. Fold in remaining sugar. Fit the pipe into the piping bag and fill with the meringue. Pipe a close zig-zag over the top of each banana, using all the meringue, and stand them on the baking tray again. Increase the oven heat to hot (220 c, 425 f, gas 7) and bake the bananas for about 5 minutes to set the meringue. Serve immediately.

Makes 6

Calculator

(Illustrated opposite)

Metric		Imperial
50 g	**butter, softened**	2 oz
125 g	**soft brown sugar**	4 oz
150 g	**self-raising flour**	5 oz
1.25 ml	**bicarbonate of soda**	$\frac{1}{4}$ teaspoon
1	**egg**	1
2	**ripe bananas**	2
2.5 ml	**vanilla essence**	$\frac{1}{2}$ teaspoon
100 g	**Cadbury's Dairy Milk Chocolate**	$3\frac{1}{2}$ oz
40–60 ml	**milk**	2–3 tablespoons
	Filling and icing	
1 large	**Cadbury's Flake**	1 large
1 packet	**dessert topping mix**	1 packet
125 ml	**cold milk**	$\frac{1}{4}$ pint
60 ml	**Cadbury's Drinking Chocolate**	3 tablespoons
1 large packet	**Cadbury's Buttons**	1 large packet
28 × 18-cm	**cake tin, greased and base lined**	11 × 7-in
1	**greaseproof paper piping bag**	1
	plain writing pipe	
	large board or tray	

Store the completed cake in the refrigerator because of the creamy icing. This cake is easier to make on a cool day as the topping can become rather runny if it is very hot.

Measure the bicarbonate of soda carefully as a little too much can give this delicious, easy cake an unpleasant taste.

Use a potato masher to mash the butter, sugar, flour and bicarbonate of soda with the egg, bananas and essence together in a bowl until the mixture has no lumps and is well mixed. Cut each square of chocolate into four then mix into the cake mixture with enough milk to make a dropping consistency. Spread the mixture in the prepared tin and bake in a moderate oven (180 c, 350 f, gas 4) for about 50 minutes until cooked through. Turn out and cool on a wire tray.

Cut a 5-cm/2-in wide slice off one short side of the cake. Assemble the cake on the board, propping up the cut slice with the Flake so that it stands at an angle to one of the short ends.

Whisk the dessert topping with the milk until it holds its shape. Place two spoonfuls in the piping bag fitted with the plain writing pipe; add the drinking chocolate to the remainder, stirring it in evenly. Spread the chocolate mixture evenly all over the cake, including the sides. Pipe the figures and signs of a calculator on the Buttons with the plain topping mixture and place them in position. Pipe a plain white line round the edge to complete the cake. *Serves 12–16*

Animal Bricks (page 32), Number Biscuits (page 33) and Calculator

Animal Bricks

(Illustrated on page 31 and back cover)

Metric		Imperial
3 egg quantity plain Victoria sponge cake (page 12)		
5 ml	ground ginger	1 teaspoon
1	small lemon	1
350 g	chocolate butter icing (page 16)	12 oz
25 g	butter	1 oz
40 g	icing sugar, sifted	1½ oz
1 packet	Cadbury's Animals	1 packet
18-cm	square deep cake tin, greased and	7-in
	base lined	
	small star pipe	
1	greaseproof paper piping bag	1

The iced cakes will freeze but do not add the biscuits until the cakes are thawed again.

Make up the sponge mixture, adding the ground ginger and finely grated lemon rind to the mixture. Mix in enough lemon juice to make a soft dropping consistency. Spread the mixture in the prepared tin and bake in a moderate oven (180 C, 350 F, gas 4) for about 50 minutes until well risen and cooked. Turn out and cool on a wire tray. Cut into 9 squares.

Cover the pieces of cake with chocolate butter icing, making them as smooth and square as possible. Beat the butter and icing sugar together until soft and pale. Fit the pipe into the piping bag, fill with the icing then pipe a selection of numbers on the bricks. Stand one Animal biscuit on top of each brick cake and press others on the sides. *Makes 9*

Alphabet letters can easily be substituted for the numbers, perhaps choosing childrens' names or the animals themselves.

A good game to encourage younger children to mix at a party is to give each child an animal noise to make and encourage them to find another child making the same noise. As a reward, give the pair their Cadbury's Animal biscuits.

Mallow Fudge

(Illustrated on page 66)

Metric		Imperial
450 g	granulated sugar	1 lb
50 g	butter	2 oz
25 g	Bournville Cocoa	1 oz
40 ml	honey	2 tablespoons
200 g	condensed milk	7 oz
80 ml	water	4 tablespoons
125 g	marshmallows	4 oz
18-cm	square shallow cake tin, greased	7-in

You do not need a sugar thermometer to make this recipe. Have a saucer of *cold* water near and every so often, drop a little mixture into the water. When ready, the fudge will set quite firmly as it drops in the water. If in doubt boil for a couple of minutes longer. Beat fudge really hard to get the correct shine and silky texture.

Measure all the ingredients, except the marshmallows, into quite a large saucepan. Using a wooden spoon, stir continuously over a very low heat until *all* the sugar granules have dissolved. Slowly bring to the boil, then cook steadily, but do not burn, until the soft ball stage is reached: that is, 114 c/238 f on a sugar thermometer. Stir the mixture only occasionally. Take the pan off the heat and immediately beat really hard with the wooden spoon until the fudge thickens, is smooth and not at all grainy.

Whilst still hot, add the marshmallows to the pan, then pour the fudge into the prepared tin. The marshmallows will melt slightly and as they do, swirl them through a couple of times, leaving the pattern showing. Leave to set overnight, then cut into squares. *Makes 36 pieces*

Number Biscuits

(Illustrated on page 31)

It is important to use hard fat for this recipe otherwise the biscuits tend to spread too much during cooking. They keep well in an airtight container, but soften and crumble in the freezer – particularly if kept for a long period.

Metric		Imperial
125 g	**hard margarine or butter**	4 oz
125 g	**caster sugar**	4 oz
2	**egg yolks**	2
50 g	**ground almonds**	2 oz
125 g	**plain flour, sifted**	4 oz
30 ml	**Bournville Cocoa,** sifted	1 heaped tablespoon
	almond essence	
4	**thin angelica strips**	4
4	**glacé cherries**	4
	large nylon piping bag	
	large star pipe	
2	**baking trays, greased**	2

Cream the margarine and sugar well together; beat in the egg yolks. Mix in the almonds, flour, cocoa and a few drops of essence to taste. Fit the pipe into the piping bag, fill it with the biscuit mixture, then pipe the numbers on to the prepared trays, allowing a little space between each biscuit and making them in batches if necessary. Cut small diamonds of angelica and the cherries into eight, and arrange a few pieces of each in a small decoration on the figures. Refrigerate the biscuits for 10 minutes to allow the mixture to harden before baking in a moderate oven (180 c, 350 f, gas 4) for about 10 minutes. Cool slightly before lifting off the baking trays. *Makes 25–30 biscuits*

Pretty Maid

(Illustrated opposite)

Metric		Imperial
125 g	**soft margarine or butter, softened**	4 oz
125 g	**caster sugar**	4 oz
2	**eggs, size 2**	2
150 g	**plain flour**	5 oz
15 ml	**baking powder**	3 teaspoons
25 g	**Bournville Cocoa, sifted**	1 oz
	pink food colouring	
100 ml	**redcurrant jelly**	5 tablespoons
350 g	**plain butter icing (page 16)**	12 oz
2 small packets	**Cadbury's Buttons**	2 small packets
	china figure head	
1	**paper umbrella**	1
800-ml	**ovenproof basin, greased**	1½-pint
	flat, serrated icing pipe	
2	**greaseproof paper piping bags**	2

Cream the margarine or butter and sugar together until pale in colour and a light texture. Gradually add the eggs. Sift the flour and baking powder together, then fold into the mixture. Halve the mixture, add the cocoa to one portion and pink food colouring to the other. Place alternate spoonfuls of both mixtures in the basin, swirl through once with a spoon and hollow out the top slightly. Bake in a moderate oven (180 c, 350 f, gas 4) for about 1 hour, until well risen and cooked through. Turn out and cool on a wire rack.

Cut the cake horizontally into three layers, spread with the jelly and sandwich together again. Colour all but three spoonfuls of the butter icing pink. Cover the cake with pink icing and, using a round-bladed knife, mark flowing lines down the skirt. Carefully lift the cake on to a pretty plate. Fit the pipe into the piping bag and fill with pink icing. Pipe a little icing on top of the cake to secure the figure head in position. Pipe a neat row around the top rim of the cake as shown in the picture. Press the figure head firmly on top. Pipe a row of pink icing just above base of the cake, then pipe a row of plain butter icing overlapping it, right on to the plate, as shown in the picture. Polish the Buttons, then, lastly, arrange them in two rows, again following the picture. Push in the umbrella to complete the lady. *Serves about 8*

The cake and butter icing may be frozen if carefully packed. Add the Buttons when thawed.

The china heads are available from specialist cook's suppliers, quite often by mail order.

To obtain a different effect, make up half the frosting from the Pantomime Mice recipe (page 115), adding a little pink food colouring. Swirl the frosting over the cake to make a really pretty skirt then press on the Buttons. This method is particularly useful when you wish to avoid piping.

Pretty Maid and Cockle Shells (page 36)

Cockle Shells

(Illustrated on page 35)

Metric		Imperial
125 g	**butter**	4 oz
25 g	**icing sugar, sifted**	1 oz
125 g	**plain flour**	4 oz
40 ml	**Cadbury's Drinking Chocolate**	2 tablespoons
1 small packet	**Cadbury's Buttons**	1 small packet
225 g	**plain butter icing (page 16)**	8 oz
	pink food colouring	
5 ml	**fresh lemon or orange juice**	1 teaspoon
20 ml	**coloured sugar strands**	1 tablespoon
	icing sugar	
	large nylon piping bag	
	star vegetable pipe	
	baking tray	

It is easy to make the shell shapes smaller for younger children, making double the number of biscuits. The mixture can also be adapted into Iced Gems by making smaller individual stars, baking for about half the time then placing a Button or sugar strands in the centre whilst the biscuits are still hot.

Cream the butter, gradually adding the icing sugar. Sift the flour and drinking chocolate together and gradually add to the creamed mixture, beating until quite pliable. Fit the star pipe into the piping bag, fill with the mixture and pipe ten shell shapes on to the baking tray. Bake in a moderately hot oven (190 c, 375 f, gas 5) for 15 minutes. Immediately the biscuits are removed from the oven, press two Buttons on to the narrow end of each biscuit. Lift carefully on to a wire rack to cool.

Match the biscuits into pairs. Colour the butter icing pink and beat in the fruit juice. Spoon into the washed and dried pipe and piping bag, then pipe a generous whirl on one biscuit of each pair and sandwich together. Sprinkle with sugar strands and dust with a little icing sugar before placing on a plate. *Makes 5*

Big Ears

(Illustrated on page 59 and back cover)

Metric		Imperial
125 g	**butter**	4 oz
75 g	**caster sugar**	3 oz
1	**egg yolk**	1
75 g	**Cadbury's Bournvita**	3 oz
175 g	**plain flour, sifted**	6 oz
	Topping	
1 packet	**marshmallows**	1 packet
25 g	**butter**	1 oz
20 ml	**golden syrup**	1 tablespoon
75 g	**Bournville Dark plain chocolate**	3 oz
65 g	**'Rice Krispies'**	$2\frac{1}{2}$ oz
	Decoration	
1 packet	**Cadbury's Fingers**	1 packet
24	**silver sugar balls**	24
14 g	**flaked almonds**	$\frac{1}{2}$ oz
	heart-shaped biscuit cutter	
	baking tray, greased	
12	**deep patty tins**	12

Cream the butter and sugar together until pale and soft. Beat in first the egg yolk, then the Bournvita and flour, mixing until the ingredients form a dough. Roll out to approximately 0.5 cm/$\frac{1}{4}$ in thick and cut out the biscuits with the cutter. Space out the biscuits on the prepared baking tray and bake in a moderate oven (180 c, 350 f, gas 4) for about 15 minutes. Allow to stand on the tray until the biscuits are firm before lifting off to cool on a wire tray.

Reserve six marshmallows, then melt the remainder gently in a large pan with the butter, syrup and broken-up chocolate. When liquid, take off the heat and stir in the krispies, coating them completely. Divide the mixture between the patty tins, pressing it in slightly. Leave to set for a couple of hours in the refrigerator.

Turn out the krispie toppings and press them firmly on to the biscuits. Push two Finger biscuits in at an angle in the krispies at the wider end of each heart biscuit. Cut the marsh-mallows horizontally through the centre, then in half across. Press a silver ball into each piece of marshmallow and position these to represent eyes as shown in the picture. Complete by adding pieces of almond for teeth. *Makes about 12*

Cakes for Compliments

The most striking feature of any party tea table is the cake which forms the centrepiece and is the focal point of all the festivities. Children will delight in such features as the Bournville Belle, for instance, or Fingers Cottage and the attractiveness of the designs will win compliments from all your guests.

The Bournville Belle

(Illustrated opposite)

It is easier to wrap and freeze the iced cakes *before* they are decorated.

This is definitely a party cake as the chocolate biscuits and sweets that are part of the train cake, all add to the fun of a special occasion. The cake can be completely assembled the day before it is required and stored in a cool place overnight.

Metric		Imperial
	For the engine	
1	**unfilled chocolate Swiss roll (page 14)**	1
	For the trucks	
4	**eggs, size 2**	4
125 g	**caster sugar**	4 oz
125 g	**plain flour**	4 oz
25 g	**Bournville Cocoa**	1 oz
40 ml	**warm water**	2 tablespoons
	Decoration	
1 kg	**plain butter icing (page 16)**	2 lb
225 g	**lemon curd**	8 oz
	yellow food colouring	
40 ml	**Bournville Cocoa**	2 tablespoons
2 packets	**Cadbury's Buttons**	2 packets
4	**chocolate mini-rolls**	4
6	**Cadbury's Star Bars**	6
3 large	**Cadbury's Flakes**	3 large
125 g	**fruit pastilles**	4 oz
1 packet	**Cadbury's Fingers**	1 packet
450-g	**loaf tin, greased and base lined**	1-lb
	cotton wool	
1	**greaseproof paper piping bag**	1

Make the Swiss roll according to the recipe instructions and leave rolled up but unfilled.

Make the trucks singly, using half the ingredients for each. Whisk the eggs and sugar with an electric mixer until thick and creamy, when the mixer will leave a good trail. Sift the

The Bournville Belle and Sleepers (page 121)

39

flour with the cocoa and fold them into the mixture, with the water. Turn into the prepared loaf tin and bake the cake in a fairly hot oven (200 c, 400 f, gas 6) for 10–12 minutes until cooked. Turn the cake out on to a wire tray, clean and prepare the tin as before, then make another cake in the same way.

Prepare the large amount of butter icing with an electric mixer. Stir half the lemon curd and a little yellow colouring into two-thirds of the amount. Dissolve the cocoa to a paste with a little boiling water and blend into the remaining butter icing.

Unroll the Swiss roll, spread with lemon butter icing and roll up tightly. Following the diagrams for cutting the Swiss roll, cut off a 5-cm/2-in slice (1). Make another cut half way down through the roll 5-cm/2-in further along (2), cut horizontally through the middle of the roll, from the sliced-off end in as far as the last cut, and take out the resulting wedge (3). Stand the whole slice on the ledge to make a higher cab for the engine, and stand the smaller piece on end next to it (4). Hold all the pieces together with a little of the lemon icing, then cover the roll completely with icing. Lightly polish the Buttons and press them on to the front, sides and cab of the engine, as shown in the picture, writing the name on the front. Cut one mini-roll in half and stand these funnels on top of the engine, with a piece of cotton wool to represent smoke. Balance the engine on a halved Star Bar. Cut a mini-roll into four and place the slices in position for wheels.

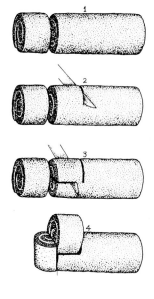

Slice the loaf cakes horizontally through the middle and sandwich them together again with the remaining lemon curd. Cover one of them completely in lemon butter icing and the other in chocolate butter icing. Press Buttons round the sides. Lay the Flakes on top of the yellow truck and pipe two thin lines of icing over the top. Pile the pastilles on the other truck. Stand the two trucks on the Star Bars in the same way as the engine and put mini-roll wheels in position. Join the engine and trucks together with Finger biscuits.

Make a track from the Sleepers (page 121), with the remaining Fingers arranged across them as railway lines.

Serves about 20

Space Invaders

(Illustrated on page 43)

It's very easy to vary the decorations for these buns using almost any Cadbury brand. This means that the latest space craze can be re-created by the youngsters in the family.

Metric		Imperial
125 g	**soft margarine**	4 oz
75 g	**caster sugar**	3 oz
125 g	**self-raising flour, sifted**	4 oz
20 ml	**Bournville Cocoa, sifted**	1 tablespoon
60 ml	**orange marmalade**	3 tablespoons
2	**eggs**	2
	Decoration	
450 g	**plain butter icing (page 16)**	1 lb
40 ml	**Bournville Cocoa**	2 tablespoons
7	**digestive biscuits**	7
1 packet	**Cadbury's Fingers**	1 packet
14	**glacé cherries**	14
2 small packets	**Cadbury's Buttons**	2 small packets
8	**Cadbury's Coasters**	8
15	**bun tins, greased**	15

Measure the margarine, sugar, flour and cocoa with the marmalade and eggs into a bowl and beat hard until all the ingredients are really well blended. Place a good teaspoonful of the mixture into each bun tin. Bake in a moderately hot oven (190 c, 375 f, gas 5) for 20–30 minutes until risen and springy to the touch. Turn out and cool on a wire tray.

Halve the butter icing. Blend the cocoa to a smooth paste with a little hot water, then mix it into one portion of the icing. Cover seven of the upside-down buns with the chocolate icing and stand each of them on a digestive biscuit. Halve two Finger biscuits and stick them round one bun, with another piece of Finger biscuit standing in the centre. Top the Fingers with halved cherries and a Button in the centre, as shown in the picture. Make the others in the same way.

Cover the base of the remaining buns with chocolate butter icing and the sides with vanilla-flavoured icing. Turn them over and stand them on the chocolate side of the Coaster biscuits. Stick four Buttons round the side of each and three halves of Finger biscuit at an angle on top. *Makes 15*

Flake 7 Rocket

(Illustrated opposite and on back cover)

Metric		Imperial
125 g	soft margarine	4 oz
125 g	soft brown sugar	4 oz
2	eggs	2
125 g	self-raising flour	4 oz
25 g	Bournville Cocoa	1 oz
1	filled chocolate Swiss roll (page 14)	1
	Decoration	
450 g	plain butter icing (page 16)	1 lb
	yellow food colouring	
25 g	Bournville Cocoa	1 oz
7	Cadbury's Flake from the Family Pack	7
	gold and silver sugar balls	
1	dariole tin, greased	1
18-cm	round shallow cake tin, greased and base lined	7-in
1	star pipe	1
3	greaseproof paper piping bags	3
23-cm	round cake board	9-in

The individual cakes may be packed and frozen, ready to assemble later.

It is important to match the size of the hole cut in the round cake with the circumference of the Swiss roll. As a guide, cut round a suitable jam jar or use a sharp plain pastry cutter.

Cream the margarine and sugar together, beat in the eggs, then fold in the flour and cocoa sifted together. Three-quarters fill the prepared dariole tin and tap it lightly on the work surface to remove any air pockets. Spread the remaining mixture in the round tin. Bake the cakes together on a baking tray in a moderately hot oven (190 C, 375 F, gas 5) for about 25 minutes; the smaller cake will take 5 minutes less. Turn out and cool. Have the Swiss roll completed.

Reserve 2 heaped tablespoons of the butter icing and colour this a deep yellow. Blend the cocoa with a little boiling water, then mix the paste into the remaining amount.

Cut a 6-cm/2¼-in circle out of the centre of the round cake and lift the ring on to the cake board. Stand the Swiss roll upright in the hole. Cover with chocolate icing. Stand the small circle of cake on the Swiss roll and sandwich the dariole cake securely on top with icing. Cover all the rocket shape with chocolate icing. Shave one end of six Flakes to stand angled against the Swiss roll.

Fit a bag with a star pipe and fill it with yellow icing, then pipe a zig-zag of neat stars round the rocket base, as shown in the picture. Pipe more butter icing round the nose cone end. Press the last Flake into the top, piping yellow and chocolate icing round its base. Finally, pipe the name in yellow icing and decorate with sugar balls. *Serves 8–12*

Flake 7 Rocket, Flying Saucer (page 44) and Space Invaders (page 41)

Flying Saucer

(Illustrated on page 43)

Metric		Imperial
	5 egg quantity chocolate Victoria sponge cake	
	(page 12)	
40 ml	**Bournville Cocoa**	2 tablespoons
500 g	**plain butter icing (page 16)**	1 lb 2 oz
1 (50-g) bar	**Bournville Dark plain chocolate**	1 (50-g) bar
8	**Cadbury's Fingers**	8
1 large	**Cadbury's Flake**	1 large
1	**Cadbury's round chocolate biscuit**	1
9	**marshmallows**	9
20-cm	**round deep cake tin, greased and base lined**	8-in
1.2-litre	**ovenproof basin, greased**	2-pint
	small star pipe	
1	**greaseproof paper piping bag**	1
23-cm	**cake board**	9-in

The cake can be frozen complete, but it may be easier to pack it without the decoration, particularly the Finger biscuits and Flake.

The cake in the basin should be cooked above the one in the tin if there is not enough room on the same shelf in the oven. Always cook the deeper mixture towards the top of the oven where the temperature is often just a little higher.

Make up the cake mixture, leaving it marbled if preferred. Spread enough mixture in the prepared tin to come about 2.5 cm/1 in high and hollow out the centre slightly. Fill the greased basin with the remaining mixture and again, hollow out the centre. Bake the cakes in a moderately hot oven (190 c, 375 f, gas 5) for 50–60 minutes. Test with a skewer to make sure the middle of the cake is cooked before turning out and cooling on a wire tray.

Blend the cocoa with a little boiling water, then mix into half the butter icing. Fit the pipe into the piping bag and fill it with the plain butter icing. Cover the flat cake with most of the remaining plain butter icing, then lift on to the board. Pipe a row of stars round the top and bottom edges. Break the chocolate into squares and space all but two of them round the sides of the iced cake as shown in the picture. Melt the two remaining squares of chocolate.

Cut the basin cake horizontally through the middle, spread with a layer of chocolate butter icing and press together again. Cover the cake with chocolate icing, then place on top of the plain iced cake. Complete the cake by pressing Finger biscuits in round the top and the Flake in the centre. Spread a little melted chocolate on the chocolate biscuit and balance it on top of the Flake. Stick the marshmallows on to the sides of the cake with more of the melted chocolate. *Serves about 16*

Hovercraft

(Illustrated on page 47)

(Illustrated on page 47)

The completed cake may be frozen for a short time but if it is to be kept for a longer period, freeze the undecorated cakes alone.

Both cakes take about the same time to cook because of the depth of the loaf tin.

A plain writing pipe may be used in the piping bag if preferred.

Metric		Imperial
	6 egg quantity plain Victoria sponge cake (page 12)	
50 g	**Bournville Cocoa**	2 oz
1	**orange**	1
1 kg	**chocolate butter icing (page 16)**	2 lb
40 ml	**orange juice**	2 tablespoons
1 small packet	**Cadbury's Buttons**	1 small packet
225 g	**royal icing (page 17)**	8 oz
	blue food colouring	
2	**fan shaped wafer biscuits**	2
½ packet	**Cadbury's Fingers**	½ packet
1 packet	**Cadbury's Milk Digestive Biscuits**	1 packet
2	**Cadbury's Flake from the Family Pack**	2
450-g	**loaf tin, greased and base lined**	1-lb
30 × 23-cm	**roasting tin, greased and base lined**	12 × 9-in
	large board	
1	**greaseproof paper piping bag**	1

Make the cake mixture with a large electric mixer or make up half at a time. Divide in half. Blend half the cocoa to a smooth paste with a little boiling water and stir this into one portion of cake mixture. Add the finely grated rind of the orange to the second portion with just enough juice to make a dropping consistency. Fill the prepared loaf tin just over half full with the chocolate mixture. Dot the remaining chocolate and orange mixtures together in the larger tin. Smooth over the top, leaving the cake marbled, and make a slight hollow in the centre. Bake both cakes in a moderately hot oven (190 C, 375 F, gas 5) for about 40 minutes. Test the cakes with a skewer to make sure they are cooked before turning out to cool.

Have the butter icing ready. Blend the 2 tablespoons orange juice into one-third of the icing. Blend the remaining cocoa with a little boiling water and add it to the larger amount of butter icing. Cut both cakes horizontally through the middle and sandwich them together with the orange-flavoured butter icing. Cut a slice about 1.25 cm/½ in thick off the end of the loaf cake and use a little butter icing to secure it on top. Cover both cakes completely with chocolate butter icing. Press Buttons round the top piece of the loaf cake.

Reserve a little royal icing then colour the remainder blue. Spread a blue border round the edge of the board, with a little in the centre. Lift the large cake on to the board and rest the smaller one on top in the centre. Mark the surface with a fork, as shown in the picture. Cover the wafer biscuits with chocolate butter icing and stand them at an angle, at one end of the cake. Fill the piping bag with white royal icing and cut off the tip. Cut six Finger biscuits in half. Pipe a large blob of icing in the centre of two digestive biscuits and a little along the flat side of the Fingers, near the cut end. Arrange the Fingers, iced side down, on the biscuit like the spokes of a wheel. Stick a Button in the centre of each and leave to dry for 30 minutes.

Pipe a name in icing on another round biscuit and place it on the top of the cake. Arrange five Fingers in a line round the middle layer of cake, then pipe three evenly spaced lines of white icing over them to represent windows. Halve the remaining round biscuits and stick them into the cake base at an angle round the sides. Finally, press the Flakes upright into the back of the cake and rest both biscuit 'propellors' against them for support. *Serves about 30*

Tanks

(Illustrated opposite)

Metric		Imperial
2 egg quantity chocolate Victoria sponge cake		
(page 12)		
350 g	**chocolate butter icing (page 16)**	12 oz
1 large packet	**Cadbury's Buttons**	1 large packet
6	**Cadbury's Flake from the Family Pack**	6
18-cm	**square cake tin, greased and base lined**	7-in

Make up the cake by the one-stage method, then spread the mixture evenly in the prepared tin. Bake in a moderately hot oven (190 c, 375 f, gas 5) for about 25 minutes until well risen and springy to the touch. Turn out and cool on a wire tray.

Cut the cake in half, then cut one-third off each piece as shown in the diagram. Spread the four pieces of cake with butter icing. Lift the smaller pieces on top of the larger ones, positioning them level with the back edge. Press five Buttons along both of the longer sides on each base cake, then tilt one more on the top for the hatch. Keep two Flakes whole and cut the others into short lengths. Arrange these like tracks along the outer edges of the base cakes, continuing over the ends as shown in the picture. Push a whole Flake into the front of the smaller pieces of cake to make a gun barrel and complete the tanks. *Makes 2 tanks each serving 4*

The cakes may be frozen when completed.

Cutting the cake

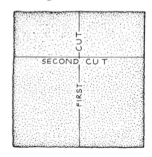

Hovercraft (page 45) and Tanks

Tracking Cake

(Illustrated on page 123)

Metric		Imperial
300 g	**soft margarine**	10 oz
300 g	**caster sugar**	10 oz
5	**eggs**	5
250 g	**self-raising flour**	9 oz
50 g	**Bournville Cocoa**	2 oz
10 ml	**baking powder**	2 teaspoons
175 g	**stoned dates, chopped**	6 oz
	Decoration	
800 g	**plain butter icing (page 16)**	1 lb 12 oz
	finely grated rind of 1 orange	
about 40 ml	**orange juice**	about 2 tablespoons
100 ml	**orange marmalade**	5 tablespoons
4	**Cadbury's Fingers**	4
2 large	**Cadbury's Flakes**	2 large
125 g	**marzipan**	4 oz
	red, green and blue food colouring	
1 small packet	**Cadbury's Buttons**	1 small packet
28 × 18-cm	**cake tin, greased and base lined**	11 × 7-in
18-cm	**square cake tin, greased and base lined**	7-in
	trefoil cocktail cutter	
	large board	

The cake will freeze complete when iced but put the tracking signs on when required. Wrap well in foil.

It is important to make the cakes the same depth in the tins so check the uncooked cake mixture with a skewer to see that it is evenly distributed before baking.

This is a cake that guides could probably make themselves and it would certainly be welcome at a guide meeting or a campfire, particularly at the end of a trail.

This cake can also be prepared by the traditional Victoria sandwich cake method.

Cutting the cakes

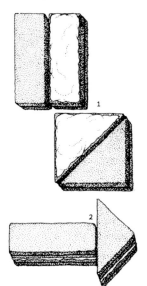

Make up the cake with a large electric mixer if possible. Place all the ingredients, except the dates, into the bowl, sifting the dry ingredients. Beat well for a good 2 minutes, then add the dates. Divide the mixture between the prepared tins and bake in a moderately hot oven (190 c, 375 f, gas 5) with the square tin above, for about 45 minutes. Cover the cakes with a piece of foil or greaseproof paper after 30 minutes to prevent them burning on top. Turn out and cool on a wire tray.

Make up the butter icing and blend in the orange rind and juice. Cut both cakes in half horizontally and sandwich together again with marmalade. Cut the oblong cake in half lengthways and the square cake in half diagonally (1). Sandwich the oblong and triangular cakes together with a little butter icing making deep cakes which fit together to form an arrow shape (2). Stick the cakes together on the board and cover them completely with the remaining icing, making it as smooth as possible.

Build a campfire of Finger biscuits on the arrow head, with some crumbs of Flake and the odd piece of marzipan, coloured red, inside. Split the Flakes into thinner pieces, reserving a big piece for the flagpole and making tracking signs with the remainder, as shown in the picture. Divide the marzipan into four and work the various colours into three portions. Roll out the marzipan and cut out two trefoil shapes of each colour, including the plain marzipan. Stick these badges in ascending order on each side of the arrow head, as illustrated. Arrange a circle of Buttons on the end of the cake, with one in the middle to represent the 'gone home' sign. Draw a World flag or substitute a Union Jack and stick it on to the Flake flagpole with a little icing. Serve slices of this cake with the traditional mug of cocoa. *Serves about 30*

Harriet Hedgehog

(Illustrated on page 23)

※

Harriet may be wrapped in foil and frozen complete. Allow at least 4 hours to thaw completely.

By popular request, this is the only idea to be reproduced from *Cadbury's Chocolate Cookbook*, though the cake is marbled this time.
To avoid tears from younger children, cut the cake into slices from the back, leaving the face intact.

Metric		Imperial
1	**pudding basin cake (page 13)**	1
350 g	**plain butter icing (page 16)**	12 oz
30 ml	**Bournville Cocoa**	1 good tablespoon
2 large packets	**Cadbury's Buttons**	2 large packets
1	**glacé cherry**	1
2	**roasted coffee beans or small sweets**	2
1.2-litre	**ovenproof basin, greased**	2-pint

Make up and bake the cake mixture as described in the recipe.

Reserve three heaped tablespoons of the butter icing. Blend the cocoa into a paste with a little boiling water or hot orange juice, then cool slightly and beat into the larger quantity of icing. Spread the flat base of the turned-out cake with half the plain icing, then cut it in half down the middle. Sandwich the two iced ends together to make the dome shape of the hedgehog. Cut down through the cake on either side of the butter icing, spread with the remaining plain icing and put the cake back together again. Lift the cake on to a board or flat plate and cover it completely with chocolate butter icing. Put a little more chocolate icing on one end and mark with a fork to make a pointed snout and face.

Rub the Buttons to make them shine, then cut each in half. Stick them in at an angle, in lines, over three-quarters of the cake leaving the forked area clear, ensuring all the Buttons point in the same direction. Place the cherry in position to make a nose and the coffee beans or small sweets on the cake to represent eyes. *Serves about 10*

Dartboard

(Illustrated opposite and on back cover)

❄
Wrap and freeze the complete cake.

🥄

If two cake tins are not available, make up all the cake mixture at once but cook the cakes separately, one after the other, in the same tin, washing it out in between.

Lemon or orange flavour butter icing tastes equally as good with the chocolate cake.

If miniature darts are not available, paper ones look most effective but they have to be stuck on with a star of butter icing.

Metric		Imperial
225 g	**butter**	8 oz
175 g	**light soft brown sugar**	6 oz
4	**eggs**	4
175 g	**golden syrup**	6 oz
225 g	**self-raising flour, sifted**	8 oz
25 g	**Bournville Cocoa**	1 oz
5 ml	**ground ginger**	1 teaspoon
5 ml	**ground mixed spice**	1 teaspoon
	Decoration	
60 ml	**apricot jam**	3 tablespoons
350 g	**plain butter icing (page 16)**	12 oz
5 ml	**ground ginger**	1 teaspoon
50 g	**Bournville Dark plain chocolate, grated**	about 2 oz
	liquorice spiral with half a glacé cherry in the centre	
	small darts (optional)	
	cake candles and holders	

2 (25-cm)	**round shallow cake tins, well greased and base lined**	2 (10-in)
30-cm	**round cake board**	12-in
	plain writing and star pipes	
2	**greaseproof paper piping bags**	2

Cream the butter and sugar together. Gradually beat in the eggs, then the syrup. Fold in the flour and divide the mixture in half. Blend the cocoa to a thick paste with boiling water and add to one portion of cake mixture. Sift the spices into the other portion, with a little orange juice or milk if necessary to make a soft dropping consistency. Spread the two mixtures separately in the prepared tins and hollow out the centres to give a cooked cake which is flat on top. Bake in a warm oven (160 c, 325 F, gas 3) for about 35 minutes until springy to the touch and cooked. The cakes are quite shallow. Turn out and leave the cakes upside down to cool. Peel off the paper.

Place an 18-cm/7-in round cake tin base or plate on each cake in turn. Using the base or plate as a guide, cut out a circle from the middle of each of the cakes with a knife (1). Lift out the centre circles then cut each with 20 even wedges, as shown in the diagram (2). Place the ginger outer ring on the cake board and arrange the coloured sections alternately, to fill the centre (3). Spread the top with jam. Lay the chocolate ring on top and repeat the process with the remaining cake, reversing the colours to get a chequered effect (4).

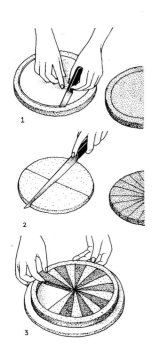

Trophy Cake (page 52), Dartboard and Dominoes (page 28)

Beat the butter icing with the ginger then spread some around the sides of the cake. Coat in grated chocolate. Attach the plain pipe to one of the piping bags, fill it with butter icing and pipe the numbers in the correct sequence and over the correct colour, round the 'board'. It's easiest to start at 20. Fit the star pipe in the remaining bag, fill it with butter icing and pipe lines of shells for the two scoring circles. Pipe a line round the top and bottom outer edges as shown in the picture. Stick the liquorice bull's eye in the centre, with the darts. Make an arrow shape from the candles to celebrate a birthday or to commemorate a sporting occasion.

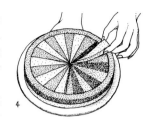

4

Trophy Cake

(Illustrated on page 50)

Metric		Imperial
125 g	**butter**	4 oz
175 g	**caster sugar**	6 oz
4	**eggs, separated**	4
80 ml	**milk**	4 tablespoons
1	**lemon**	1
125 g	**ground almonds**	4 oz
75 g	**Bournville Dark plain chocolate**	3 oz
175 g	**self-raising flour**	6 oz
	Filling	
60 ml	**black cherry jam**	3 tablespoons
	Crème au beurre and decoration	
225 g	**unsalted butter**	8 oz
4	**egg whites**	4
225 g	**icing sugar, sifted**	8 oz
100 g	**Bournville Dark plain chocolate**	$3\frac{1}{2}$ oz
20-cm	**round deep cake tin, greased and base lined**	8-in
30-cm	**square cake board (or large oblong pastry board) covered with gold foil**	12-in
	plain writing pipe	
2	**greaseproof paper piping bags**	2
	waxed paper	

Beat the butter and sugar together, then add the egg yolks and milk. Grate the lemon rind finely and keep covered to use in the cake covering. Add the strained lemon juice to the cake mixture with the ground almonds. Grate the chocolate and add it to the mixture, then stir in the flour and make sure the ingredients are well mixed. Whisk the egg whites quite

This cake keeps well and will freeze complete. Chocolate attracts moisture so it will glisten when thawed. The chocolate shapes can also be added later as they store well in an airtight container.

Chocolate Shapes
Draw or trace bold outlines of the chosen sport motifs on to a sheet of plain paper. Lay this sheet of paper flat on a board and cover with a piece of waxed paper, waxed side upwards. Pipe over the outline with melted chocolate. Try to get the chocolate at the right temperature so that it is not too thick to work. If it is too hot it will run quickly out of the bag and you will not be able to pipe the line. Leave the chocolate shapes to set completely before carefully peeling them off.

Cutting the Cake

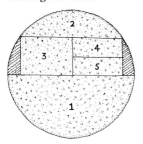

1 *Cut the cake exactly in half and cut a parallel line 5 cm/2 in from the straight edge of one half.*

2 *Trim the remaining piece to make straight ends then cut it in half. Cut one half into two more pieces.*

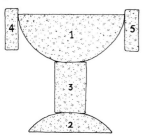

3 *Arrange the pieces of cake as shown.*

The roll freezes well – to do so, wrap the roll first in its greaseproof paper, then in foil.

stiffly and fold in carefully. Turn the mixture into the tin and bake in a warm oven (160 c, 325 f, gas 3) for about 1¼ hours. Turn out and cool on a wire tray.

Slice the cake horizontally through the middle and sandwich it back together with jam. Follow the diagram to cut the cake correctly; start by cutting the cake in half and then cut the pieces as shown. Assemble the pieces on a large board, again carefully following the diagrams.

In a bowl, soften the butter for the crème au beurre. Whisk the egg whites and icing sugar together in a basin over a pan of hot water. Whisk until the mixture is white, thick and holds its shape. Continue whisking off the heat for a few minutes, then beat in the soft butter, a spoonful at a time. Add the reserved lemon rind. Remove 2 good tablespoonfuls and spread the rest evenly over the cake, all except the base.

Melt the chocolate in a bowl over a pan of hot water. Fit the plain writing pipe into the piping bag and put two small spoonfuls of the white icing into the bag. Mix about one-third of the chocolate into the remaining icing; cover the base cake with chocolate icing. Use the white icing to pipe the words, as shown in the picture. Decorate with chocolate shapes made from the remaining Bournville Dark. *Serves about 16*

Jigsaw Roll

(Illustrated on page 126)

Metric		Imperial
75 g	**butter**	3 oz
75 g	**caster sugar**	3 oz
20 ml	**Bournville Cocoa**	1 tablespoon
1 packet	**Cadbury's Shorties**	1 packet
1	**egg, size 2**	1
1 packet	**marshmallows**	1 packet
about 50 g	**icing sugar**	about 2 oz

large, double piece of greaseproof paper

Melt the butter in quite a large saucepan and stir in the sugar and cocoa. Crush the biscuits roughly, leaving quite large pieces, then stir them into the butter mixture with the egg. Leave the mixture in the pan until cool and beginning to set.

Using a pair of scissors, cut the marshmallows into four pieces and stir into the chocolate mixture. Sift the icing sugar on to the greaseproof paper, then turn the biscuit mixture out on to it. Form into a 20-cm/8-in long roll using the paper to help you. Wrap up well then chill overnight. Unwrap the roll and cut it into slices. *Makes 12–14 slices*

Feather Bonnet

(Illustrated opposite)

Basket decoration

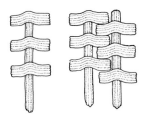

Start the basket pattern at the back of the cake where any mis-shapen lines are not likely to be noticed among the feathers. Basket work is quite easy to do and covers the cake surface remarkably quickly but if you have not tried the pattern before, practise on a clean work surface. Use only one colour of icing to practise with as the two colours, once piped together, cannot be separated to use again.

Metric		Imperial
	4 egg quantity plain Victoria sponge cake	
	(page 12)	
40 ml	**Bournville Cocoa**	2 tablespoons
2.5 ml	**vanilla essence**	$\frac{1}{2}$ teaspoon
	pink food colouring	
40 ml	**red jam**	2 tablespoons
	Decoration	
800 g	**plain butter icing (page 16)**	1 lb 12 oz
	pink and yellow food colourings	
1 packet	**marshmallows**	1 packet
2	**mimosa sugar balls**	2
	angelica	
	feathers	
1.2-litre	**ovenproof basin, greased**	2-pint
24-cm	**round deep cake tin, greased and**	$9\frac{1}{2}$-in
	base lined	
	star and ribbon icing pipes	
2–4	**greaseproof paper piping bags**	2–4
30-cm	**round plate or cake board**	12-in

Make up the cake mixture then divide it into three equal portions. Add the cocoa to one amount, vanilla to a second and colour the third portion pink. Fill one-third of the basin with a little of each of the three mixtures and put the rest in the prepared tin. Do not stir the mixtures together but leave the separate colours to show attractively when the cake is cut. Smooth lightly over the top. Bake the cake in the basin above the tin in a moderately hot oven (190 c, 375 f, gas 5) for about 50 minutes until cooked through and risen. Turn out and cool on a wire tray.

Spread the top of the basin cake with jam then turn it over and press it on top of the round cake, slightly off centre. Stand the cake on the plate.

Colour 450 g/1 lb of the butter icing with pink colouring and the remainder pale yellow. Fit the star pipe into a piping bag and fill with the yellow icing. Fit a larger bag with the ribbon pipe and fill with pink icing. Using the two pipes alternately, pipe a line of yellow icing down the crown of the hat and cross it with small lines of basket weave, leaving even gaps, as shown in the diagram. Continue to make the pattern until the whole crown of the hat is covered. Do the same for the hat brim, re-filling the bags as often as necessary. Pipe a ribbon line of yellow icing.

Feather Bonnet, Flower Tubs (page 25) and Flower Power (page 73)

Place a marshmallow on the top of the hat where the icing lines meet. Halve the remaining marshmallows horizontally to make them thinner, then cut these in half again and arrange alternate colours round the bottom edge of the cake as shown in the picture. Make two simple flowers from the marshmallows, with stars of butter icing and mimosa balls in the centre and a few angelica leaves. Stand the feathers in the back of the cake at a jaunty angle. *Serves about 20*

Mushroom Manor

(Illustrated on page 18)

Metric		Imperial
40 ml	**Bournville Cocoa**	2 tablespoons
225 g	**soft margarine**	8 oz
225 g	**caster sugar**	8 oz
60 ml	**orange marmalade**	3 tablespoons
4	**eggs, separated**	4
300 g	**self-raising flour, sifted**	10 oz
	Moulding paste	
80 ml	**liquid glucose**	4 tablespoons
2	**egg whites**	2
1 kg	**icing sugar, sifted**	2 lb
	yellow and green food colouring	
about 120 ml	**apricot jam, warmed**	about 6 tablespoons
	Decoration	
40 ml	**royal icing (page 17)**	2 tablespoons
	sugar flowers	
1 large packet	**Cadbury's Buttons**	1 large packet
	Cadbury's Drinking Chocolate	
1.2-litre	**ovenproof basin, greased**	2-pint
19-cm	**round cake tin, greased and base lined**	7½-in
4-cm	**round pastry cutter**	1½-in
	plain writing pipe	
1	**greaseproof paper piping bag**	1

Freeze the plain cakes and decorate them when required.

Use a warm spoon to measure liquid glucose accurately.

It is quite easy to make the paste in an electric mixer. Carefully hold a clean tea towel taut over the machine to stop the icing sugar flying all over the kitchen.

Keep the moulding paste wrapped in a polythene bag once it is coloured so that it does not dry out. It the paste becomes too firm to work comfortably, sprinkle on a few drops of water and knead it again.

Dissolve the cocoa in a little boiling water. Cream the margarine and sugar together well, then beat in the dissolved cocoa and the marmalade. Add the egg yolks, then fold in the flour. Whisk the egg whites quite stiffly and fold in evenly. Fill the greased basin about three-quarters full with cake mixture, then spread the rest in the prepared tin. Bake in a warm oven (160 C, 325 F, gas 3) for about 1¼ hours. Test with a skewer to see that both cakes are cooked through. Turn out and cool on a wire tray.

Prepare the moulding paste by gradually blending the glucose and egg whites into the icing sugar. When there is no icing sugar left, knead the paste into a ball. Dust a work surface lightly with icing sugar and continue kneading until the paste is smooth and pliable. Divide the paste in half and knead a little yellow colouring into one portion and green into the other, making sure the colours are delicate.

Cut the round cake horizontally in half and sandwich it together with half the apricot jam. Brush both cakes all over with the remaining jam. Roll out both the coloured pastes in turn. Mould the yellow paste over the basin cake and the green paste over the round sponge, including just enough green paste to tuck neatly under the edge. Use the pastry cutter and a sharp knife to cut out a door shape and five windows from the yellow paste.

Place the round cake on top of the basin cake and lift carefully on to a suitable plate or board. Fit the pipe into the piping bag and fill it with the royal icing. Pipe the windows and round the door, pressing some flowers on to make it look really pretty. Pipe a little icing on the back of the lightly polished Buttons and arrange them over the green cake, with a few more for the path. Sift a little drinking chocolate on top of the cake. *Serves 16–20*

Flake Envelopes

(Illustrated on page 78)

Metric		Imperial
225 g	**marzipan**	8 oz
	red and green food colouring	
	caster sugar	
1	**Cadbury's Flake Family Pack**	1

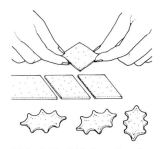

Make fairly thick flat strips of green marzipan, then cut out diamond shapes about 2.5 cm/1 in. in length. Pinch the ends and edges for the holly leaf points and twist them so that they curl up realistically. Leave the leaves to dry for a short time.

Knead the marzipan until soft, then roll out quite thinly on a sugared surface. Cut into 6.5-cm/$2\frac{1}{2}$-in squares, working the scraps together to roll and cut out again in between, making 18 squares in all. Colour a small amount of the remaining marzipan bright red and a slightly larger piece green. Roll very small amounts of the red marzipan into holly berries then coat them in sugar. Roll out the green marzipan into a flat sheet and cut into narrow strips, as illustrated, to make the leaves. Pinch out the edges of the leaves to represent holly.

Lay a Flake diagonally across each marzipan square and fold up the corners, pressing them together over the Flake. Press a marzipan holly leaf and berries on to each as shown in the picture. Sprinkle with sugar. *Makes 18*

White Rabbit

(Illustrated opposite)

Metric		Imperial
25 g	**Bournville Cocoa**	1 oz
150 g	**self-raising flour**	5 oz
2.5 ml	**baking powder**	$\frac{1}{2}$ teaspoon
175 g	**soft margarine**	6 oz
175 g	**caster sugar**	6 oz
3	**eggs, size 2**	3
	Decoration	
450 g	**plain butter icing (page 16)**	1 lb
	pink and green food colouring	
225 g	**desiccated coconut**	8 oz
4	**Cadbury's Buttons**	4
2	**silver sugar balls**	2
1	**glacé cherry**	1
1	**liquorice shoe lace**	1
	marzipan carrots (below)	
	ribbon bow	
2 (22-cm)	**shallow round cake tins,**	2 (8½-in)
	greased and base lined	
	large board	

Sift the dry ingredients together for the cakes, then beat in the margarine, sugar and eggs, creaming all the ingredients together really well. Divide the mixture equally between the tins. Bake the cake in a moderately hot oven (190 C, 375 F, gas 5) for 25–30 minutes until well risen and cooked. Turn out and cool on a wire tray. Cut the cakes, carefully following the diagrams.

Mix a few drops of pink colouring into two spoonfuls of coconut. Press plain coconut all over the cake and make the inside of the ears and hind paws out of the pink coconut. Position the two Button eyes and use a little icing to stick a silver ball on each, add the cherry 'nose'. Cut various lengths of liquorice for feet, eyebrows, mouth and finally, long whiskers. Place the marzipan carrots on one paw and the ribbon bow on the neck with the remaining Buttons down the centre of the cake.

Any remaining coconut may be coloured green and sprinkled round the edge of the cake. *Serves about 16*

Carrots Work orange food colouring into 50 g/2 oz marzipan, then divide it into three or four pieces. Roll and shape the marzipan into carrots, mark the surface with short lines and stick pieces of angelica into the end.

The complete cake can be carefully wrapped and frozen for a short time.

To cut the cake

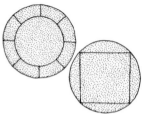

1 *Start by cutting a 4-cm/1½-in wide ring, measured from the outer edge of one cake then cut this ring into eight pieces.*

2 *Make a 16-cm/6½-in square from the other cake, cutting all the cake neatly so that no bits are wasted.*

3 *Halve both large pieces horizontally and sandwich together with butter icing. Place the round piece above the square one on a large board and proceed to assemble the rabbit shape as shown. Stick all the pieces together with butter icing before covering the cake completely with most of the remaining icing.*

White Rabbit and Big Ears (page 37)

58

Anniversary Cake

(Illustrated on page 15 and front cover)

Metric		Imperial
50 g	**Bournville Cocoa**	2 oz
175 g	**self-raising flour**	6 oz
2.5 ml	**bicarbonate of soda**	½ teaspoon
good pinch	**salt**	good pinch
125 g	**soft margarine**	4 oz
225 g	**dark soft brown sugar**	8 oz
2	**eggs**	2
150 g	**natural yogurt**	5 oz
2.5 ml	**vanilla essence**	½ teaspoon
	Filling and frosting	
100 ml	**redcurrant jelly**	5 tablespoons
2	**egg whites**	2
350 g	**icing sugar, sifted**	12 oz
1.25 ml	**cream of tartar**	¼ teaspoon
80 ml	**water**	4 tablespoons
	Decoration	
about 15	**sugar bells (opposite)**	about 15
40 ml	**thick glacé or royal icing**	2 tablespoons
	(page 17), coloured yellow	
2 (19-cm)	**round shallow cake tins,**	2 (7-in)
	greased and base lined	
1	**greaseproof paper piping bag**	1
	appropriate coloured ribbon	
23-cm	**round plate or cake board**	9-in

The complete cake may be frozen but be careful to put it on a board or plate suitable for cold temperatures.

The frosting keeps the cake moist and it can therefore be made a couple of days in advance.

This cake can be decorated with any colour icing and ribbon; for example pink or blue for a christening or yellow for a golden wedding anniversary.

Sift all the dry ingredients for the cake into a bowl. Add all the remaining ingredients and beat for a good three minutes until thoroughly mixed. Divide the mixture between the prepared tins. Bake in a moderately hot oven (190 c, 375 f, gas 5) for about 35 minutes until well risen and cooked. Turn out and cool on a wire tray.

Split both cakes in half, then spread the bottom layer of each with redcurrant jelly and sandwich together again. Do not put the two cakes on top of each other.

Prepare the frosting by measuring all the ingredients into quite a large bowl and standing it over a pan of hot water. Beat, preferably with an electric hand mixer, until stiff peaks form and the icing is satin smooth and white, which will usually take 8–10 minutes. Spread some frosting over one cake, then sandwich the two together to make one deep cake. Without picking up any crumbs on the knife, spread the cake liberally with frosting; cover it completely leaving definite swirls and peaks. Carefully lift the cake on to the plate.

Before the frosting sets, arrange a pattern of sugar bells on top. Pipe bows of yellow icing on the edge and arrange an attractive bow of ribbon in the centre (paper ribbon stands up particularly well).

Sugar Bells

Small metal bells are usually available in different sizes at large department stores, particularly around Christmas time. Take out the piece in the middle so that a bell mould shape remains. Clean thoroughly before using.

The dry sugar bells keep well in a clean dry place.

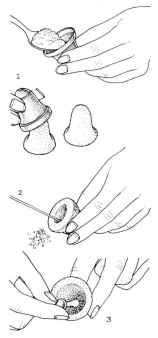

Metric		Imperial
125 g	**granulated sugar**	4 oz
40 ml	**royal icing (page 17),**	2 tablespoons
	coloured yellow	
	mimosa sugar balls	
	metal bell shapes	
1	**greaseproof paper piping bag**	1

Put the sugar in a bowl and carefully add only about three or four drops of water, making the sugar just moist. Be very careful not to add too much water. Pack the sugar into the bell moulds as tightly as possible then tap it out on to a clean surface (1). Use up all the sugar in the same way. Leave the bells long enough for the sugar on the outside to harden enough to handle.

When the outside is hard, lift the bell very carefully and with a skewer, scrape out the soft sugar inside, leaving a hard bell-shaped shell (2). It is important to catch the sugar before it is too hard in the centre of the bells. Leave all the shells to dry completely.

Put the icing into the piping bag then pipe a line in the middle of each bell. Stick a mimosa (or silver) sugar ball on each one (3). *Makes 15–30 bells, depending on size*

Daisy Cream Cake

(Illustrated opposite)

Metric		Imperial
4	**eggs, separated**	4
150 g	**icing sugar**	5 oz
65 g	**plain flour**	2½ oz
14 g	**cornflour**	½ oz
25 g	**Bournville Cocoa**	1 oz
2.5 ml	**baking powder**	½ teaspoon
a few drops	**vanilla essence**	a few drops
	Filling and icing	
142 ml	**whipping cream**	¼ pint
60 ml	**redcurrant jelly**	2 good tablespoons
350 g	**plain butter icing (page 16)**	12 oz
	pink food colouring	
8	**white marshmallows**	8
4	**mimosa sugar balls**	4
4	**thin pieces angelica**	4
10 ml	**icing sugar**	2 teaspoons
20-cm	**round loose-based deep cake tin, greased and base lined**	8-in
	baking tray	

This is a particularly light, fresh cream cake so it should be kept in a cool place once made. The combination of flavours is delicious.

Put the egg yolks into a large bowl, sift in the icing sugar, then beat really well until pale and fluffy. Whisk the egg whites stiffly and fold in carefully. Sift the dry ingredients together and fold in carefully with the essence and a little milk if the mixture is too stiff. Turn the mixture into the prepared tin and level the surface by tilting it gently. Bake on the tray in a moderate oven (180 c, 350 f, gas 4) for 40–45 minutes until cooked and springy to the touch. Cool in the tin.

Whip the cream and sieve the redcurrant jelly into it. Slice the cake into three even layers and sandwich them together again with the cream. Colour the icing pale pink and spread it all over the cake, marking smooth lines on the top and the sides with a fork or serrated cake scraper. Slice the marshmallows horizontally, then cut each piece in half. Arrange them in flower shapes on top with a mimosa ball in the centre. Cut the angelica to fit down the side of the cake and place two pieces of marshmallow at the bottom of each strip to make leaves. Sprinkle icing sugar in the centre just before serving. *Serves 8*

Sweetheart Surprise (page 24), Cupid Biscuits (page 112) and Daisy Cream Cake

Fingers Cottage

(Illustrated on page 27)

Metric		Imperial
4 egg quantity chocolate Victoria sponge cake		
(page 12)		
	Butter icing	
300 g	**butter or soft margarine**	10 oz
450 g	**icing sugar, sifted**	1 lb
25 g	**Bournville Cocoa**	1 oz
	Decoration	
2 packets	**Cadbury's Fingers**	2 packets
	sugar flowers	
1	**silver sugar ball**	1
	angelica diamonds	
6	**deep bun tins, greased**	6
18-cm	**square deep cake tin, greased**	7-in
	star pipe	
3	**greaseproof paper piping bags**	3
	large board	

Make up the cake mixture following the recipe, making a dropping consistency. Half fill the greased bun tins, then put the remaining mixture into the prepared square tin. Hollow out the centre slightly. Bake the cakes in a moderate oven (180 C, 350 F, gas 4), allowing about 25 minutes for the small cakes and 50–60 minutes for the large one. Turn out and cool on a wire try.

To make the butter icing, cream the butter and beating really hard, add the icing sugar. Take out and reserve two good tablespoonfuls. Blend the cocoa to a paste with boiling water and mix evenly into the larger quantity of butter icing.

Cut the cake as shown in the diagram. Slice the large piece horizontally through the middle and sandwich it back together with some of the icing. Cover the top and sides of the cake with icing, then place the two triangular pieces on top so that they form a pointed roof, as shown in the diagram. Spread butter icing over this too and make sure the whole cake is neat. Cut two Finger biscuits in half, then stand them upright in the centre of the roof, to make a chimney. Lay a Finger biscuit flat on either side of the chimney, along the top of the roof, then arrange the remaining biscuits in lines down the slope of the roof, covering the ends of the cake neatly. Lift the cake on to a suitable sized board or tray.

Fill a piping bag with the reserved butter icing. Pipe a door and windows on the cottage and press on the sugar flowers. Pipe a door knob and press in the silver ball. Press

The cottage may be wrapped loosely and frozen for about a month.

Cutting the cake

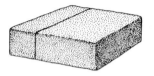

1 *Cut a 7.5-cm/3-in strip off one side of the cake.*

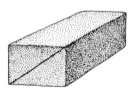

2 *Cut this strip diagonally in half, making 2 long triangular pieces.*

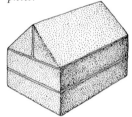

3 *Slice the large piece of cake horizontally through the middle. The triangular strips form the roof when the cake is sandwiched together.*

The cottage also looks attractive with white walls (vanilla butter icing) and chocolate doors and windows.

Winter Log Cabin
A winter log cabin (illustrated on front cover) may easily be made in the same way substituting 9 large, halved, Cadbury's Flakes for the Fingers on the roof and using Christmas decorations instead of the flowers.

a Finger biscuit under each of the end windows and arrange flowers on them to represent window boxes.

Pipe circles of different coloured butter icing on the top of each of the little cakes. Spread the sides with any remaining butter icing and stand halved Finger biscuits round them. Decorate with angelica and a few more sugar flowers if available. Arrange these flower barrels round the cottage.

Fairy Castle

(Illustrated on page 15)

Shave the chocolate with a warm, sharp knife and it will be quite easy to get a good shape. Store the bits of chocolate in a screw topped jar and use to decorate a dessert or cake.

Metric		Imperial
1	**unfilled chocolate Swiss roll (page 14)**	1
40 ml	**black cherry or blackcurrant jam**	2 tablespoons
142 ml	**whipping cream, whipped**	$\frac{1}{4}$ pint
$\frac{1}{2}$ quantity	**frosting for Anniversary Cake (page 60)**	$\frac{1}{2}$ quantity
	pink food colouring	
2 (20-g) bars	**Cadbury's Dairy Milk Chocolate**	2 small bars
	silver sugar balls	
18-cm	**round silver cake board**	7-in
1	**greaseproof paper piping bag**	1
	plain writing pipe	
2	**silver doilies**	2

Make the Swiss roll; roll it up from the long side, without the filling, and leave to cool. Later, spread the inside with jam and whipped cream, then roll up again to make a long roll. Cut into three pieces measuring about 15-cm/6-in, 10-cm/4-in and 5-cm/2-in.

Make up the frosting according to the recipe instructions. Take out one-third and colour this a delicate pink, then swirl it on the cake board. Spread the white frosting all over the three pieces of Swiss roll and stand them upright in a triangle shape on the board. Cut each bar of chocolate into five pieces. Fill the piping bag with a little frosting and pipe a small square window and door knob on one piece of chocolate. Press a silver ball on to the door knob and press into position on the smallest piece of cake. Shave the remaining pieces of chocolate to a point at one end and pipe a trellis on them for windows. Decorate with silver balls and stick these windows in position around the castle cake. Cut the doilies in half and shape into cones, fastening them with sticky tape, then place the three turrets in position. A little fluffed-out cotton wool could be put round the cake on the table. *Serves about 8*

Cadbury's Chocolate Box

(Illustrated opposite)

✑

To test if the sugar syrup has reached the short thread stage, dip a wooden spoon into the pan. Lightly oil your fingers and pinch a little of the syrup off the spoon, pulling it away so that it comes away in short threads. If the syrup does not form threads then boil and test again.

Metric		Imperial
100 g	**Bournville Dark plain chocolate**	3½ oz
60 ml	**boiling water**	3 tablespoons
175 g	**butter**	6 oz
175 g	**caster sugar**	6 oz
5 ml	**vanilla essence**	1 teaspoon
4	**eggs, separated**	4
25 g	**Bournville Cocoa**	1 oz
200 g	**self-raising flour**	7 oz
	Sugar syrup	
50 g	**granulated sugar**	2 oz
125 ml	**water**	scant ¼ pint
20 ml	**maraschino liqueur**	1 tablespoon
175 g	**black cherry jam**	6 oz
	Moulding paste	
25 g	**Bournville Cocoa**	1 oz
450 g	**icing sugar**	1 lb
20 ml	**glucose syrup**	1 tablespoon
5 ml	**glycerine**	1 teaspoon
60–80 ml	**maraschino liqueur**	3–4 tablespoons
	Cadbury's Drinking Chocolate	
	Decoration	
350 g	**royal icing (page 17)**	12 oz
	green food colouring	
1 large packet	**Cadbury's Buttons**	1 large packet
	sugared flowers	
225 g	**Rose's Milk Chocolates**	8 oz
22-cm	**square deep cake tin, greased and fully lined**	8½-in
20 × 8-cm	**stiff card, covered in foil**	8 × 3-in
	star and plain writing pipes	
2	**greaseproof paper piping bags**	2

Melt the chocolate in a small pan with the water. Cream the butter, sugar and essence until light in colour and texture. Fold in the egg yolks and melted chocolate, then the cocoa and flour sifted together. Add a little milk if necessary to give the correct soft consistency. Whisk the egg whites until stiff then fold them into the mixture and turn it into the prepared tin, hollowing out the centre slightly. Bake in a moderate oven (180 c, 350 f, gas 4) for about 1 hour until risen and firm to the touch. Turn out and cool on a wire tray.

Cadbury's Chocolate Box, Mallow Fudge (page 32) and Praline Swirls (page 120)

67

Dissolve the sugar in the water for the sugar syrup and when quite clear, boil rapidly for about three minutes until the short thread stage is reached. Stir in the liqueur and allow to cool. Pour the cool syrup over the cake.

Cut the cake in half horizontally to give two layers, then cut each layer in half again, vertically across the middle to make four rectangles. Spread two of them with half the jam, then sandwich three layers together, leaving the fourth for the lid. Brush all the cake, including the lid, with jam.

To make the moulding paste, sift the cocoa and icing sugar into a bowl. Stir in the glucose syrup and glycerine with enough liqueur to make a mouldable paste. The easiest way to complete the mixing, though messy, is with your hands. Cut off one-third of the paste and keep it moist in a polythene bag. Dust a clean work surface with drinking chocolate and roll the larger portion of paste into a thin strip 12 × 65 cm/5 × 25 in or make two shorter pieces if it is easier. Wrap the rolled-out paste round the sides of the large piece of cake, taking it just over the top edge and smoothing it carefully with your fingers to make it as even as possible. Roll out the remaining paste to fit the lid, covering the top, sides and overlapping underneath. Place this piece of cake on the foil covered card.

Mark even diagonal lines about 2.5 cm/1 in apart on the paste, as a guide for piping. Colour the royal icing pale green. Fit the pipes in the two piping bags and fill them both with the royal icing. Pipe plain lines over the marks on the paste, making diamond shapes. Where the piped lines cross, pipe a small star of icing and press on alternate Buttons and flowers before the icing dries. Lift the base cake on to an oblong plate. Pipe a shell edging round the lid and cake base. Cover the top of the cake with a selection of Rose's chocolates and the home-made sweets, then prop the lid on top as shown in the picture. Leave the icing to dry before serving the cake.

Serves about 16

Sugared flowers

To make sugared flowers, choose fresh dry edible flowers such as primroses or violets. Many spring flowers are suitable.

1 *Lightly whip one egg white in a bowl and paint this over each individual petal.*

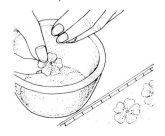

2 *Dust the flower with caster sugar, separating each petal, using a paint brush to help coat them completely. Leave the flowers to dry in a sunny warm place for a day. Store in a clean dry place, ready to use as required.*

Circus Ring

(Illustrated on page 114)

❄

The cake will freeze.

Hollow out the cake mixture so that you can almost see the tin itself in the centre. With slow cooking, the cake should be quite flat, which is important for the appearance.

Metric		Imperial
125 g	**butter**	4 oz
125 g	**caster sugar**	4 oz
2	**eggs**	2
50 g	**plain flour**	2 oz
50 g	**self-raising flour**	2 oz
25 g	**Bournville Cocoa**	1 oz
50 g	**hazelnuts, finely chopped**	2 oz
25 g	**desiccated coconut**	1 oz
2.5 ml	**vanilla essence**	½ teaspoon
about 60 ml	**milk**	about 3 tablespoons
	Icing	
40 ml	**blackcurrant cordial**	2 tablespoons
125 g	**plain butter icing (page 16)**	4 oz
	pink food colouring	
1 large packet	**Cadbury's Buttons**	1 large packet
20-cm	**fluted flan tin, greased and base-lined**	8-in
1	**greaseproof paper piping bag**	1
	star pipe	
	candle holders and candles	
	toy animals	

Cream the butter and sugar together until pale in colour and light in texture. Gradually beat in the eggs, then sift together the flours and cocoa and fold into the mixture. Stir in the remaining ingredients with sufficient milk to give a soft dropping consistency. Spread the mixture in the tin, hollowing out the centre really well and bake on a baking tray in a warm oven (160 c, 325 f, gas 3) for about 1 hour. Turn out the cake to cool on a wire tray.

Carefully spoon the cordial over the flan base to soften it and lift on to a plate. Add a little colouring to the butter icing. Fit the pipe into the piping bag and fill with the butter icing. Pipe a row of overlapping shells on the rim of the flan. Lay the Buttons flat on the top and sandwich two together for the centre as shown in the picture. Arrange suitable circus animals in the ring with any other appropriate figures, such as toy clowns. Keep in a cool place until required.

Serves about 8

Soldier Boy

(Illustrated opposite)

Metric		Imperial
1	**unfilled chocolate Swiss roll**	1
	(page 14)	
350 g	**plain butter icing (page 16)**	12 oz
2 large	**Cadbury's Flakes**	2 large
	red food colouring	
40 ml	**Bournville Cocoa**	2 tablespoons
1 small packet	**Cadbury's Buttons**	1 small packet
4	**digestive biscuits**	4
10 ml	**desiccated coconut**	2 teaspoons
25 g	**marzipan**	1 oz
2	**pieces flaked almonds**	2
1	**greaseproof paper piping bag**	1
	cake board	

The filled Swiss roll may be frozen but it is probably best to complete the decoration just before it is to be used.

With care, the cake will remain upright for several hours, supported by the large Flake inside the Swiss roll and the firm biscuits.

Add red colouring slowly as it tends to darken on standing.

Prepare the Swiss roll according to the recipe instructions. Spread with some of the butter icing then lay a Flake along one short end and roll up the Swiss roll. Colour 75 g/3 oz of the butter icing red for the jacket, then blend the cocoa with boiling water before adding to the remaining icing.

Cover the top and bottom third of the roll with chocolate butter icing and the centre section with red icing, making it neat and smooth. Press two Buttons in the centre. Put a little red icing into the piping bag, cut off the tip and pipe a face on the top portion. Either pipe on a chin strap, or use a piece of red liquorice.

Sandwich the biscuits together with butter icing and spread a little round the edge. Roll the edge in coconut. Spread both ends of the biscuit pile with icing. Stand the decorated Swiss roll upright on the cake board. Arrange the pile of biscuits sideways as a drum, helping to support the 'soldier'. Press Buttons on to the drum sides and as feet for the soldier. Cut the Flake into smaller pieces; keep two thin pieces as drum sticks and arrange the rest round the top of the Swiss roll as a busby hat, making the top and bottom lines as even as possible.

Colour the marzipan red, then roll into two thin pieces and stick it on to the cake to represent arms. Press pieces of almond into the end of the arms and balance the Flake drum-sticks in position. *Serves 6–8*

Soldier Boy and Birthday Parade (page 81)

Butterfly Cake

(Illustrated on page 27)

Metric		Imperial
	3 egg quantity chocolate Victoria sponge cake	
	(page 12)	
1	**small orange**	1
	Decoration	
225 g	**icing sugar, sifted**	8 oz
	orange food colouring	
2 squares	**Bournville Dark plain chocolate,**	2 squares
	melted	
2 packets	**Cadbury's Buttons**	2 packets
350 g	**plain butter icing (page 16)**	12 oz
25 g	**Bournville Cocoa**	1 oz
1 large	**Cadbury's Flake**	1 large
1	**glacé cherry**	1
2	**thin strips angelica**	2
19-cm	**round deep cake tin, greased**	7½-in
	and based lined	
1	**greaseproof paper piping bag**	1
25-cm	**round cake board**	10-in

Wrap loosely and pack the complete cake carefully in the freezer. Keep for about a month.

To test if a deep cake is cooked, carefully insert a warm skewer into the middle of it. When it is cooked through to the base, the skewer will come out clean. Cool on a wire tray.

Make up the cake mixture, adding the finely grated orange rind and about half the juice, to make a dropping consistency. Spread the mixture in the prepared tin and hollow out the centre slightly. Stand the tin on a baking tray and bake in a moderate oven (180 c, 350 f, gas 4) for 65–70 minutes. Turn out and cool completely on a wire tray.

Cut the cake into three equal layers and decorate the top one first. Use the icing sugar and remaining orange juice left from the cake to make a stiff glacé icing, adding more water if necessary. Colour the icing orange (or yellow) and make it quite a stiff coating consistency. Fill the piping bag with the warm melted chocolate and cut just the tip off the bag. Spread the icing smoothly over the cake, letting it flow over the edge. Pipe a spiral design of chocolate as shown in the diagrams for Cobweb Cake. Draw a skewer outwards from the centre eight times. Immediately cut the cake in half and put a Button on each half as shown in the picture.

Divide the butter icing in half. Blend the cocoa to a paste with a little boiling water and add to one amount. Colour the other half with a little orange colouring. Spread the chocolate butter icing all over one of the remaining layers of cake, including the sides. Mark the top in a spiral with a fork and press polished Buttons all round the side. Place this layer on the cake board.

Cover the remaining sponge with the orange butter icing. Cut in half and arrange the semi-circles back to back, covering about two-thirds of the chocolate base as shown in the picture. Cover the cut edges with butter icing and build up a little icing on the 'wing' ends. Mark straight lines with a fork over the top and sides. Spread orange butter icing on the cut edges of the feather iced cake. Balance the two halves, again back to back, on top of the orange sponge. Rest the Flake down the centre, add a glacé cherry for the head and place the angelica in position. *Serves about 16*

Flower Power

(Illustrated on page 54)

❋

The cake may be wrapped and frozen with the icing and coconut on it. Add the biscuits and sweets when the cake is thawed.

Metric		Imperial
175 g	**butter or margarine**	6 oz
175 g	**caster sugar**	6 oz
3	**eggs, size 2**	3
175 g	**self-raising flour, sifted**	6 oz
25 g	**desiccated coconut**	1 oz
1	**orange**	1
	Icing and decoration	
60 ml	**Cadbury's Chocolate Spread**	3 tablespoons
500 g	**plain butter icing (page 16)**	1 lb 2 oz
50 g	**desiccated coconut**	2 oz
1 packet	**Cadbury's Milk Assorted Biscuits**	1 packet
50 g	**small jelly sweets**	2 oz
23-cm	**round cake tin, greased and base lined**	9-in

Cream the butter and sugar well together until pale and soft. Beat in the eggs one at a time, adding a spoonful of the flour if the mixture shows any signs of curdling. Fold in the flour and coconut with the finely grated orange rind and just enough juice to make a soft dropping consistency. Spread the mixture evenly in the tin. Bake in a moderately hot oven (190 c, 375 f, gas 5) for about 30 minutes until well risen and springy to the touch. Turn out to cool on a wire tray.

Cut the cake horizontally through the middle and sandwich together again with chocolate spread. Spread the icing smoothly all over the cake, covering the sides too. Immediately press on the coconut and lift the cake on to a large plate or cake board. Decorate with an arrangement of biscuits and sweets as shown in the picture.

Country Cake

(Illustrated on title spread and opposite)

Metric		Imperial
250 g	**soft margarine**	9 oz
175 g	**Cadbury's Drinking Chocolate**	6 oz
140 g	**caster sugar**	4½ oz
3	**eggs**	3
75 g	**self-raising flour, sifted**	3 oz
75 g	**seedless raisins**	3 oz
	Fudge topping	
125 g	**butter**	4 oz
120 ml	**Cadbury's Drinking Chocolate**	6 tablespoons
100 ml	**milk**	5 tablespoons
350 g	**icing sugar, sifted**	12 oz
	Decoration	
25 g	**desiccated coconut**	1 oz
	green food colouring	
1 packet	**Cadbury's Fingers**	1 packet
	small toy tractor and scarecrow	
	green cake candles and holders	
28 × 18-cm	**shallow cake tin, greased and base lined**	11 × 7-in
	rectangular board	

The cake and topping may be frozen. Add the coconut and biscuits later.

The texture of the fudge topping depends on the beating so use an electric hand mixer in the pan, if you have one.

To colour coconut Dampen the coconut slightly before rubbing in food colouring with your fingers. It's messy but effective. Spread on a baking tray and either dry on a sunny shelf or in a low oven for up to 30 minutes. Store in an airtight container for a short time.

Melt 75 g/3 oz of the margarine, then stir in the drinking chocolate; cool. Cream the remaining margarine and sugar together, gradually beat in the eggs with a spoonful of the flour. Fold in the remaining flour, raisins and drinking chocolate mixture. Turn the cake into the prepared tin, spreading it evenly. Bake in a moderate oven (180 c, 350 f, gas 4) for about 50 minutes until risen and cooked. Carefully turn the cake out on to a wire tray and peel off the paper.

Melt the butter for the topping with the drinking chocolate and milk in a pan. Cool and chill in the refrigerator before beating in the icing sugar. Lift the cake on to a board then cover it all over with the chocolate topping. Using a wide-pronged fork, mark furrows on top of half the cake to represent a ploughed field. Colour the coconut with the green food colouring and sprinkle it over the other half.

Leave two Finger biscuits whole and cut a quarter off all the others. Make a fence by standing the larger pieces at intervals round the cake and slanting the smaller pieces in between. Stand the whole biscuits upright at one end with pieces of biscuit sideways between them to make a gate. Add the tractor, scarecrow and candles. *Serves 10–15*

Clarence Caterpillar (page 20), Country Cake and Artillery Cannons (page 117)

Merry-Go-Round

(Illustrated on page 126)

Metric		Imperial
175 g	soft margarine	6 oz
175 g	light soft brown sugar	6 oz
3	eggs	3
200 g	self-raising flour	7 oz
75 g	Cadbury's Drinking Chocolate	3 oz
50 g	walnuts, chopped	2 oz
20 ml	coffee essence	1 tablespoon
100 g	Cadbury's Dairy Milk Chocolate	3½ oz
	Icing and decoration	
400 g	plain butter icing (page 16)	14 oz
25 g	ground almonds	1 oz
2 packets	Cadbury's Fingers	2 packets
1 large	Cadbury's Flake	1 large
1 packet	Cadbury's Animals	1 packet
.40 ml	royal icing (page 17)	2 tablespoons
1 packet	Cadbury's Buttons	1 packet
15	silver sugar balls	15
20-cm	round deep cake tin, greased and lined	8-in
7	wooden cocktail sticks	7
	paper canopy	
75 cm	red ribbon	30 in
	star pipe	
1	greaseproof paper piping bag	1

Cream the margarine and sugar together until soft and light, then gradually stir in the eggs. Sift the flour and drinking chocolate together and fold them into the mixture with the walnuts and coffee essence, making a soft dropping consistency. Cut each square of chocolate into six, then fold the pieces into the cake. Turn the mixture into the tin, hollow out the centre slightly and bake the cake in a moderate oven (180 c, 350 f, gas 4) for about 1¼ hours. Turn out and cool on a wire tray.

Prepare the butter icing and beat in the ground almonds. Cover the top and sides of the cake with this icing, forking over the top. Lift the cake on to a large flat plate or board. Lightly polish the Finger biscuits before pressing them upright against the side of the cake. Stand the Flake in the centre, pressing it in firmly. Stick six Animal biscuits on to cocktail sticks and arrange them near the cake edge, at different heights to resemble a merry-go-round. Stand more Animals round the Flake. Prepare the paper canopy according to the instructions.

Freeze the cake without the biscuits and canopy.

If coffee essence is not available, dissolve 15 ml/3 teaspoons instant coffee in a very little hot water and add to the cake mixture.

To make a paper canopy

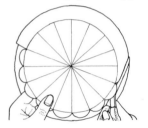

1 *Draw a 20-cm/8-in circle on to some coloured card. On the reverse side, mark the circle into 16 equal segments.*
Cut out a scalloped edge slightly away from the drawn circle.

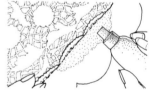

2 *Stick the doily on to the right side, with a little glue.*

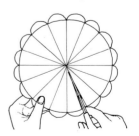

3 *Turn the card over and cut up one line in towards the centre of the circle. Glue down one complete segment.*

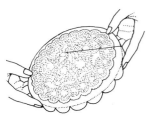

4 *Make a sharp fold round the scalloped edge. Cut out a triangular paper flag.*

Fit the star pipe into the piping bag and spoon the royal icing into it. Pipe a large star of icing on top of the Flake then one on each of the Buttons. Press on a silver ball. Pipe a star on the scalloped edges of the prepared canopy, press on the Buttons and balance the canopy on the Flake in the centre – as the royal icing sets, it will become firm. Stick a paper flag on a cocktail stick in the top and secure the ribbon round the cake to complete the merry-go-round. *Serves 12–16*

Mini Mountains

(Illustrated on page 82)

Open freeze the complete cakes. Wrap carefully, label and freeze for up to a month.

An individual cake would make a welcome small gift for someone living alone. They also look very nice as part of an edible Christmas table decoration.

Metric		Imperial
50 g	**butter, softened**	2 oz
50 g	**light soft brown sugar**	2 oz
1	**egg**	1
50 g	**self-raising flour**	2 oz
30 ml	**mincemeat**	1 good tablespoon
	Decoration	
225 g	**chocolate butter icing (page 16)**	8 oz
3 large	**Cadbury's Flakes**	3 large
50 g	**marzipan**	2 oz
	red and green food colouring	
4 (125-ml)	**individual round moulds, greased**	4 (4–5-fl oz)

Beat the butter, sugar, egg and flour together thoroughly, then stir in the mincemeat. Divide the mixture equally between the moulds, place them on a baking tray and bake in a moderate oven (180 c, 350 f, gas 4) for 20–25 minutes. Turn out and cool on a wire rack.

Spread the cakes with the butter icing. Using a sharp knife, cut the Flakes into small neat pieces and press on to the cakes as shown in the picture. Dust with icing sugar.

Work red colouring into one-third of the marzipan and green colouring into the remaining portion. Roll small pieces of red marzipan into balls. Roll out the green marzipan and make holly leaves as described on page 57. Arrange leaves and berries on top of each little cake. Lift the cakes on to individual paper plates or arrange them together attractively on a board. *Makes 4*

Treasure Chest

(Illustrated opposite)

Assemble the cake no longer than the day before it is required as the outside pieces may bend and soften a little.

To measure syrup accurately, use a hot metal spoon.

Cutting the biscuit mixture

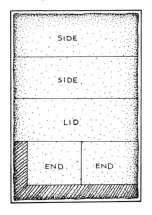

Treasure Chest, Pirates' Puddings (page 28), Loot Biscuits (page 116) and Flake Envelopes (page 57)

Metric		Imperial
2 egg quantity chocolate Victoria sponge cake		
(page 12)		
50 g	**butter**	2 oz
150 g	**soft brown sugar**	5 oz
80 ml	**golden syrup**	4 tablespoons
175 g	**self-raising flour**	6 oz
50 g	**Bournville Cocoa**	2 oz
20 ml	**milk**	1 tablespoon
	Decoration	
250 g	**lemon flavoured butter icing (page 16)**	9 oz
450 g	**royal icing (page 17)**	1 lb
1 packet	**Cadbury's Buttons**	1 packet
	silver sugar balls	
selection of pretty sweets or Loot Biscuits (page 116)		
and Flake Envelopes (page 57)		
23-cm	**square deep cake tin, greased**	9-in
	and base lined	
23.5 × 33-cm	**Swiss roll tin, greased**	9½ × 13½-in
1	**greaseproof paper piping bag**	1
	small star pipe	
28-cm	**square cake board**	11-in

Make the sponge cake first and spread the mixture in the prepared square tin. Bake in a moderately hot oven (190 c, 375 f, gas 5) for about 30 minutes until well risen and cooked. Turn out and cool on a wire tray.

Melt the butter, sugar and syrup in a saucepan. Meanwhile, sift the flour with the cocoa. Cool the butter mixture before beating in the sifted flour and cocoa with enough milk to make a stiff dough. Wrap the dough in cling film or a butter paper and leave in the refrigerator for 30 minutes. Later, roll out the biscuit dough to fit the Swiss roll tin. Bake in a moderate oven (180 c, 350 f, gas 4) for 10–15 minutes until cooked.

Cut up the warm chocolate biscuit mixture, while it is still in the tin, to the following sizes. For the long sides and the lid, cut three pieces each measuring 23 × 7.5 cm/ 9 × 3 in. For the ends of the treasure chest, cut two smaller pieces each measuring 10 × 7.5 cm/4 × 3 in.

Assemble the chest by first cutting the cake vertically in half, then slice each oblong piece horizontally through the middle. Spread with butter icing and sandwich the layers together again, putting all four layers on top of each other.

Cut the end off a piping bag and drop in the pipe. Fill with royal icing. Place the oblong cake in the centre of the cake board and build the biscuit round it, sticking the edges together with stars of royal icing. Support the biscuit pieces if necessary until the icing hardens or put a dab of icing on the cake itself. Decorate one edge of the biscuit lid with stars of icing, the Buttons and silver balls, propping it up until the icing dries.

Fill the centre of the chest with a selection of sweets or Loot Biscuits and Flake Envelopes.

Attach the lid with a row of icing stars and make a lock shape on the front.

Loch Ness Monster

(Illustrated on page 119)

Metric		Imperial
175 g	**butter or margarine**	6 oz
125 g	**caster sugar**	4 oz
	grated rind of 1 orange	
75 g	**black treacle**	3 oz
3	**eggs**	3
150 g	**self-raising flour**	5 oz
25 g	**Bournville Cocoa**	1 oz
	Icing	
65 g	**butter**	2½ oz
60 ml	**milk**	3 tablespoons
80 ml	**Cadbury's Drinking Chocolate**	4 tablespoons
225 g	**icing sugar, sifted**	8 oz
	Decoration	
2	**chocolate mini rolls**	2
1	**round Cadbury's biscuit**	1
3 or 4	**small pieces of angelica**	3 or 4
1	**glacé cherry**	1
2	**pieces flaked almonds**	2
15-cm	**round deep cake tin, greased and base lined**	6-in
	large board or tray covered with coloured foil paper	

The iced cake may be frozen but thaw carefully as the icing tends to become very moist.

It is important to beat the icing really hard and an electric mixer is ideal for this. The thickness and gloss of the finished icing will depend on the beating.

Make the cake by creaming the butter, sugar and orange rind together until soft and light. Beat in the treacle, then the eggs, one at a time. Sift the flour and cocoa together and fold into the mixture, ensuring no pockets of flour are left. Turn into the prepared tin and bake in a moderate oven (180 C, 350 F, gas 4) for about 1 hour 10 minutes, until reasonably firm but not overcooked. Turn out carefully and cool on a wire tray. Peel off the greaseproof paper when cold.

To make the icing, melt the butter, milk and drinking chocolate together in a pan. Allow to cool before beating in the icing sugar until fairly thick and quite smooth.

Slice the cake horizontally into three equal layers, then sandwich two together again with a little of the icing. Halve the remaining layer of cake, then sandwich together with a little icing, making a semi-circle. Cut the large cake into two, making one piece quite a lot larger than the other, ending up with a total of three different sized pieces of cake. Cover each piece with icing, making the surface rough. Arrange the pieces of cake on the tray, in a line or semi-circle, cut sides down as shown in the picture. Cut one mini roll diagonally in half with a sharp knife and cover one piece with icing. Place in position for the tail. Cover the remaining halved and whole mini rolls with icing, then assemble both on top of the biscuit to form a head, as shown. Stick in a crest of angelica, 2 slices of glacé cherry for eyes and the almonds sticking out behind. The Monster is now ready to eat. *Serves about 12*

Birthday Parade

(Illustrated on page 71)

The iced cake may be frozen but the Finger biscuits are more difficult to stick on to hard icing. It may be necessary to make up a little more chocolate butter icing to coat the sides before pressing on the biscuits, or spread with apricot jam.

Soldier candle holders can be bought from some newsagents or department stores. If they are the wrong colour, paint over them with a permanent ink pen.
Before pressing them on to the cake, rub Finger biscuits gently in your hands to remove any loose chocolate and give a good shine.

Metric		Imperial
2 egg quantity chocolate Victoria sponge cake (page 12)		
350 g	**chocolate butter icing (page 16)**	12 oz
2 packets	**Cadbury's Fingers**	2 packets
18-cm	**round deep cake tin, greased and base lined**	7-in
	candles and soldier candle holders	
	sentry box and a toy soldier	

Make up the chocolate sponge cake according to the recipe instructions and spread the mixture evenly in the prepared tin. Bake in a warm oven (160 c, 325 f, gas 3) for 35–40 minutes. Turn out and cool on a wire tray.

Slice the cake in half and spread about one-third of the butter icing in the centre before sandwiching together again. Cover the top and sides of the cake with the remaining icing. Mark the top into lines with a small palette knife. Lift the cake on to a plate or board before pressing the Finger biscuits upright on to the side. Arrange the appropriate number of candles in their soldier holders in lines on the cake and stand the toy soldier in the sentry box. *Serves about 16*

Seasonal Style

Every seasonal feast calls for a celebration cake and the exciting ideas in this chapter will appeal to all the family. There are special themes for Easter and Christmas and even Chocolate Cat motifs suitable for a Hallowe'en party – a host of good ideas to celebrate the seasonal mood.

Santas

(Illustrated opposite)

The uniced, whole or cut cake may be frozen.

Coloured icing darkens on standing so do not worry if it looks rather pink at first. To get a good result, spread the icing with a small palette knife and do not lift the knife off the surface at all until completely coated. This helps prevent the cake crumbs mixing into the soft icing.

Cutting the cake

Chimney Christmas Cake (page 84), Santas, Mini Mountains (page 77) and Star Sparkles (page 85)

Metric		Imperial
40 ml	**Bournville Cocoa**	2 tablespoons
75 g	**self-raising flour**	3 oz
2.5 ml	**baking powder**	$\frac{1}{2}$ teaspoon
125 g	**soft margarine**	4 oz
125 g	**caster or soft brown sugar**	4 oz
25 g	**ground almonds**	1 oz
2	**eggs**	2
	Decoration	
450 g	**icing sugar, sifted**	1 lb
	bright red food colouring	
2	**glacé cherries**	2
20 cm	**round cake tin, greased and base lined**	8-in
1	**greaseproof paper piping bag**	1

Sift the cocoa, flour and baking powder into a bowl, then beat in the soft margarine, sugar, ground almonds and eggs. Beat the mixture for a good 2 minutes until really well mixed, then spread it evenly in the prepared tin. Bake in a moderately hot oven (190 c, 375 f, gas 5) for 25–30 minutes until cooked. Turn out and turn the cake over to avoid marks on top. Cool.

Reserve about 75 g/3 oz of the icing sugar, then blend the remainder with enough red food colouring and water or fruit juice, to make a strong-coloured, coating glacé icing. Cut the cake into 6 wedges and cut off the bases to make triangles, (see diagram). Coat each cake with icing; dry, then trim the edges.

Use the remaining icing sugar with a little water or lemon juice to make a stiff glacé icing, fill the piping bag with this icing. Cut off just the tip of the bag and pipe a face and the line of buttons on each Santa. Cut the hole a little larger to mark the wavy lines and a blob for a hat at the top. Stick a thin piece of cherry in each and leave to dry. *Makes 6*

Chimney Christmas Cake

(Illustrated on page 82)

Metric		Imperial
225 g	**plain flour**	8 oz
40 ml	**Bournville Cocoa**	2 tablespoons
7.5 ml	**baking powder**	1½ teaspoons
5 ml	**ground mixed spice**	1 teaspoon
175 g	**butter**	6 oz
175 g	**soft brown sugar**	6 oz
4	**eggs**	4
450 g	**mixed dried fruit**	1 lb
50 g	**blanched almonds, chopped**	2 oz
50 g	**glacé cherries, quartered**	2 oz
50 g	**chopped mixed peel**	2 oz
40 ml	**rum, sherry or fruit juice**	2 tablespoons
	Decoration	
675 g	**icing sugar, sifted**	1½ lb
10 ml	**glycerine**	2 teaspoons
3	**egg whites**	3
225 g	**Cadbury's Fingers (about 1½ packets)**	8 oz
	Father Christmas figure	
	Christmas cake decorations	
16-cm	**deep square cake tin, greased and lined**	6½-in
25-cm	**square cake board**	10-in

The cake itself may be wrapped and frozen but the icing and decorations should only be added when the cake is to be used.

Do not remove the paper lining from fruit cakes if they are to be stored; it helps to keep them moist. Peel off the paper just before use.

Sift the dry ingredients together. Cream the butter and sugar, then gradually beat in the eggs with a spoonful of flour. Stir in all the remaining cake ingredients, mixing well to make a dropping consistency that is not too stiff. Turn the mixture into the prepared tin and hollow out the centre. Stand the tin on a baking tray and bake in the centre of a warm oven (160 c, 325 f, gas 3) for about 2 hours until cooked through. Cool in the tin.

Use the icing sugar, glycerine and egg whites to make up the royal icing as described on page 17. Secure the cake on to the centre of the board with a little icing, then cover both the cake and board, leaving the icing standing in peaks. Place eight Finger biscuits horizontally on each side, as shown in the picture. Encourage the icing to flow over the top biscuits.

Arrange a circle of halved Fingers on the top of the cake. Leave the icing to dry before putting the Father Christmas in position in the middle of the Finger chimney. Add the cake decorations.

This cake is not a rich fruit cake so it should be eaten within a fortnight.

Star Sparkles

(Illustrated on page 82)

These biscuits are quite effective hung on a Christmas tree but should be placed high enough to be out of the way of dogs or small children. For extra brightness, stick a silver sugar ball on each point.

Metric		Imperial
125 g	**butter**	4 oz
75 g	**caster sugar**	3 oz
1	**egg yolk**	1
225 g	**plain flour, sifted**	8 oz
50 g	**Cadbury's Bournvita**	2 oz
	Icing	
25 g	**Cadbury's Bournvita**	1 oz
175 g	**icing sugar, sifted**	6 oz
75 g	**coloured sugar crystals**	3 oz
	star-shaped biscuit cutter	
2	**baking trays, greased**	2
7 metres	**gold coloured string**	8 yards

Cream the butter and sugar together until pale and soft, then beat in the egg yolk. Add the flour, then the Bournvita and mix until the mixture forms a dough. Roll out on a lightly floured surface to about 3 mm/$\frac{1}{8}$ in thick. Cut out the biscuits; the exact number will depend on the size of your cutter. Place the biscuits slightly apart on the baking trays and bake in a moderate oven (180 c, 350 f, gas 4) for about 10 minutes. With a skewer, carefully make a hole in each warm biscuit, big enough for the string to go through later. Cool on a wire tray.

Dissolve the Bournvita for the icing in two spoonfuls of boiling water. Gradually blend in the icing sugar, making a smooth, fairly thick icing. Spread the icing neatly on each biscuit, taking it right up to the points. Sprinkle on the coloured sugar and leave to dry. Thread a piece of cord through each biscuit so that they can be hung on the Christmas tree. Store in an airtight container. *Makes about 30*

Forest Fruit Cake

(Illustrated opposite)

Metric		Imperial
175 g	**butter**	6 oz
175 g	**caster sugar**	6 oz
3	**eggs, size 2**	3
175 g	**plain flour, sifted**	6 oz
5 ml	**baking powder**	1 teaspoon
50 g	**ground almonds**	2 oz
1	**small orange**	1
75 g	**Cadbury's Dairy Milk Chocolate**	3 oz
75 g	**glacé cherries**	3 oz
50 g	**glacé pineapple**	2 oz
50 g	**chopped mixed peel**	2 oz
50 g	**sultanas**	2 oz
	Decoration	
400 g	**chocolate butter icing (page 16)**	14 oz
5 large	**Cadbury's Flakes**	5 large
	ribbon decoration	
18-cm	**deep round cake tin, greased and lined**	7-in

Wrap the complete cake in foil and freeze for up to a month.

Clean and dry fruit should always be used when making any type of fruit cake. If cherries are sticky, wash them and leave to dry before use.

Cream the butter and sugar together. Gradually beat in the eggs, then fold in the flour and baking powder with the ground almonds. Finely grate the orange rind, and add to the cake mixture. Squeeze out the juice. Cut each square of chocolate into four. Chop the cherries and pineapple quite roughly. Mix all the fruit and chocolate into the mixture with enough orange juice to make a fairly stiff dropping consistency. Spoon the mixture into the prepared tin and level the surface, slightly hollowing out the centre. Place the tin on a baking tray and bake the cake in a moderate oven (180 c, 350 f, gas 4) for 1–1½ hours until cooked through. Allow to cool a little in the tin before turning out on to a wire tray. Later, peel off the greaseproof paper.

Cover the cake liberally with the chocolate butter icing and mark the top into rings with a fork. Lift the cake on to an attractive flat plate or board. Cut the Flakes into thinner pieces, keeping them as long as possible. Carefully press upright pieces of Flake on to the side of the cake, mixing the large and smaller pieces to resemble the bark of a tree – this is remarkably realistic. Dust with sifted icing sugar and place a neat bow on top.

Forest Fruit Cake, Festive Yule Log (page 89) and Christmas Tree Biscuits (page 88)

Christmas Tree Biscuits

(Illustrated on page 87 and front cover)

Metric		Imperial
125 g	**plain flour, sifted**	4 oz
25 g	**ground almonds**	1 oz
50 g	**caster sugar**	2 oz
125 g	**butter**	4 oz
20 ml	**Bournville Cocoa**	1 tablespoon
20 ml	**Cadbury's Drinking Chocolate**	1 tablespoon
	Decoration	
120 ml	**icing sugar, sifted** 3 heaped tablespoons	
	green and red food colouring	
25 g	**coloured sugar balls**	1 oz
7	**Cadbury's Flake from the Family Pack**	7
225 g	**marzipan**	8 oz
	Christmas tree biscuit cutter	
1	**baking tray, greased and floured**	1
1	**greaseproof paper piping bag**	1

The undecorated biscuits may be frozen, or stored in an air-tight container for a short time.

Draw a pointed triangle on cardboard, making it fit the centre of the tree shape. Allow at least 0.5 cm/¼ in from the edge or else the uncooked mixture could break. Use the cut-out cardboard shape for all the biscuit centres.

The biscuit dough can be made in one colour for speed. The plain mixture could be flavoured with a little finely grated lemon or orange rind.

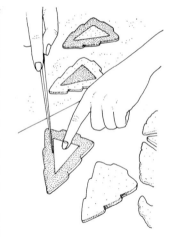

Measure 100 g/3 oz of the flour into a bowl. Add the ground almonds and sugar, then rub in the butter until the mixture resembles breadcrumbs. Divide the dry mixture in half. Knead the extra flour into one amount and the sifted cocoa and drinking chocolate into the other. On a lightly floured surface, roll out the mixtures in turn to a thickness of about 0.5 cm/¼ in. Cut out as many trees as possible, using the tree cutter, making an even number in both colours. Cut out a triangle of mixture from the middle of each biscuit, then interchange the triangular centres to alternate the colours. Press the pieces lightly together and transfer the biscuits to the baking tray. Bake in a moderate oven (180 c, 350 f, gas 4) for about 12 minutes until cooked. Leave the cooked biscuits to harden and cool a little before lifting them off the tray.

Mix the icing sugar with just enough water or lemon juice and a few drops of green colouring to make a fairly stiff glacé icing. Fill the piping bag with the icing, cut off the tip, then pipe zig-zag lines on each tree to represent the coloured lights. Press on the sugar balls. Cut each Flake into three equal pieces and use a dot of icing to secure a piece of Flake to the base of each biscuit tree. Leave to set for about an hour.

Knead a little red colouring evenly into the marzipan, then roll out to about the same thickness as the biscuits. Cut into strips measuring 6 cm/2¼ in. in length and about 2 cm/¾ in wide, making the same number as there are biscuits. Wrap the marzipan round the base of the Flake and biscuit, with the join at the back. The trees should now stand up. *Makes about 20*

1 *To halve Flake, cut across the middle with a sharp knife in one definite movement.*

2 *Split the Flake lengthways to make thinner strips. Put the point of a plain sharp knife between the grooves and press gently but evenly.*

Stand the paper cases in a tray of patty tins as they are easier to fill when the paper cannot bend too much.

Festive Yule Log

(Illustrated on page 87)

Metric		Imperial
1	**unfilled chocolate Swiss roll (page 14)**	1
300 g	**plain butter icing (page 16)**	10 oz
10	**Cadbury's Flake from the Family Pack**	10
25 g	**Bournville Cocoa**	1 oz
	icing sugar	

Make up the Swiss roll and spread the inside with just under half the butter icing. Lay two Flakes along one short end, then roll up the cake as tightly as possible. Blend the cocoa to a paste with a little boiling water, then mix into the remaining butter icing, but do not make it too stiff. Cover the length of the roll with the soft icing, leaving the ends uncovered. With a sharp knife, cut off a good slice of cake at an angle and secure it on one side of the roll with a little icing. Assemble the cake on a plate or square cake board. Cut the Flakes into smaller pieces (see diagram) and neatly press them into the icing, ensuring that all the pieces lie in the same direction. Sprinkle the Flake crumbs over the top to fill any gaps and dust with icing sugar. *Serves 6*

Crispie Nests

(Illustrated on title spread and page 95)

Metric		Imperial
50 g	**butter**	2 oz
1 packet	**marshmallows**	1 packet
125 g	**'Rice Krispies'**	4 oz
225 g	**Cadbury's Mini-Eggs**	8 oz
18	**paper cake cases**	18

Melt the butter and marshmallows slowly in quite a large pan. When melted and mixed, stir in the krispies and coat them completely in the marshmallow mixture. Divide the mixture evenly between the paper cases pressing it together slightly. Make a hollow in the centre with the back of a spoon, then leave to get quite cold before filling with mini-eggs.

Makes 18

Easter Celebration Cake

(Illustrated on title spread and opposite)

Metric		Imperial
4	**eggs, separated**	4
1	**lemon**	1
150 g	**icing sugar, sifted**	5 oz
75 g	**plain flour**	3 oz
25 g	**cornflour**	1 oz
120 ml	**apricot jam**	6 tablespoons
125 g	**marzipan**	4 oz
	yellow food colouring	
350 g	**plain butter icing (page 16)**	12 oz
10	**Cadbury's Flake from the Family Pack**	10
20-cm	**deep round cake tin, greased**	8-in
	and base lined	
	star vegetable pipe	
	small star pipe	
	nylon piping bag	
2	**greaseproof paper piping bags**	2

Pack, label and freeze complete for up to a month.

To ensure that the decoration is even, giving a more professional finish, pipe the loops at each quarter of the cake before filling in the loops between.

If a quicker decoration is preferred, crumbled Flake can be used to coat the sides of the cake.

Beat the egg yolks with the finely grated lemon rind, half the strained juice and the icing sugar until pale and fluffy. Carefully fold in the stiffly beaten egg whites, then the flours, sifted together. Pour the mixture into the prepared tin and bake in a moderate oven (180 C, 350 F, gas 4) for about 45 minutes until the sponge springs back when touched. Turn out and cool on a wire tray.

Cut the cake in half and sandwich it together again with half the jam. Mark a 7.5-cm/3-in circle in the centre of the cake with a skewer, then spread the remaining jam over the outside ring, leaving the centre clear. Soften the marzipan with enough lemon juice to give a piping consistency. Fill the nylon bag, with the large pipe attached, with the marzipan then pipe 16 loops round the inner circle, as shown in the picture. Place the cake under a hot grill for a few minutes to brown lightly and cook the marzipan.

Beat a little yellow colouring into the prepared butter icing, then spread it quite liberally over the sides of the cake, using about two-thirds of the icing. Lift the cake on to a plate or board. Halve the Flakes, then shave them into smaller pieces to stand round the edge of the cake, pressing them in well. Fit the smaller star pipe in a piping bag and pipe an edge of the remaining icing on the cake. Decorate with Easter decorations.

Valentine Spectacular (page 92) and Easter Celebration Cake

90

Valentine Spectacular

(Illustrated on page 91)

Metric		Imperial
6	**eggs, separated**	6
225 g	**icing sugar, sifted**	8 oz
1	**orange**	1
50 g	**cornflour**	2 oz
150 g	**plain flour**	5 oz
	Decoration	
80 ml	**Cadbury's Chocolate Spread**	4 tablespoons
80 ml	**seedless raspberry jam**	4 tablespoons
350 g	**plain butter icing (page 16)**	12 oz
	pink food colouring	
12	**Cadbury's Flake from the Family Pack**	12
350 g	**royal icing (page 17)**	12 oz
80 ml	**glacé icing (page 17),**	4 tablespoons
	coloured pink	
18-cm	**round deep cake tin, greased**	7-in
	and base lined	
18-cm	**square deep cake tin, greased**	7-in
	and base lined	
	small star pipe	
	star vegetable pipe	
1	**nylon piping bag**	1
1	**greaseproof paper piping bag**	1
35-cm	**heart-shaped or round cake board**	14-in
1	**rose**	1

The complete cake may be frozen. Wrap carefully. Allow at least 4 hours for the cake to thaw.

This is not really a difficult cake to prepare but it needs time, particularly for the decoration. It's worth practising the loops on the kitchen surface first. The finish is all important. Pipe the loops at all four quarters first and space the others evenly in between.

For ease, plain butter icing may be piped round the edge instead of the royal icing, but the white royal icing gives a particularly attractive, crisp finish and enhances the overall look of the cake.

Warming the chocolate spread makes it easier to spread on the soft sponge.

Whisk the egg yolks, icing sugar, finely grated orange rind and the strained juice until fluffy and pale in colour. Whisk the egg whites to the soft peak stage and carefully fold them into the yolks together with the flours, sifted together. Divide the mixture equally between the prepared tins and bake in a moderate oven (180 c, 350 f, gas 4) for about 25 minutes, until well risen and cooked. Turn out and cool the cakes on wire trays.

Cut the cakes horizontally through the centre and fill them with chocolate spread. Sandwich together again. Cut the round cake in half. Arrange the square cake diagonally on the board, with the semi-circles at the top. (See Sweetheart Surprise page 24) Stick the cakes together with a little jam. Mark out a heart shape in the centre of the cake, making it 8 cm/3 in. in from the outside edge. Spread this wide outer border with the remaining jam.

Colour the butter icing pink. Fit a large nylon piping bag with the vegetable pipe and fill it with butter icing. Pipe loops of butter icing over the jam as shown in the picture. Spread the cake sides with the remaining butter icing. Halve all but one of the Flakes, then cut them into thin strips with a sharp knife. Press the cut Flakes upright round the edge of the cake, using all the very small pieces too. Using the small pipe fitted in the greaseproof paper piping bag, pipe a shell edge of royal icing round the inside heart. Cover the loop ends and top and bottom cake edges. Flood the centre with glacé icing. Allow to set. Complete the cake by arranging the whole Flake and a rose on top. *Serves about 16*

Bunny Biscuits

(Illustrated on page 99)

To get a particularly shiny, golden finish, add an egg yolk to the milk when brushing over the biscuits.

Metric		Imperial
75 g	**butter**	3 oz
75 g	**caster sugar**	3 oz
1	**egg**	1
	finely grated rind of 1 orange	
225 g	**self-raising flour**	8 oz
2.5 ml	**ground mixed spice**	$\frac{1}{2}$ teaspoon
50 g	**currants**	2 oz
40 ml	**milk**	2 tablespoons
50 g	**Bournville Dark plain chocolate**	2 oz
1 large packet	**Cadbury's Buttons**	1 large packet
	rabbit-shaped biscuit cutter	
2	**baking trays, greased**	2
	paint brush	

Cream the butter and sugar together until pale and soft, then beat in the egg and orange rind. Sift in the flour and mixed spice, then mix in the currants. Mix well to make a pliable dough, knead quickly then roll out on a lightly floured surface to just under 1 cm/$\frac{1}{4}$ in thick. Cut out shapes with the cutter, rolling the dough trimmings again in between. Arrange the biscuits on the prepared trays and bake carefully in a moderate oven (180 c, 350 f, gas 4) for 10 minutes only.

Brush the biscuits with milk, then return them to the oven for a further 10 minutes until crisp and nicely coloured. Be careful that the edges are not too brown. Lift off and cool.

Melt the chocolate in a small bowl. With the paint brush, brush all the ears, then the paws of the bunny biscuits with chocolate. Dab a little on the tails and stick on a Button. *Makes about 24*

Easter Egg Cake

(Illustrated opposite)

Metric		Imperial
I	**pudding basin cake (page 13)**	1
	almond essence	
	pink food colouring	
	Decoration	
550 g	**plain butter icing (page 16)**	1 lb 4 oz
20 ml	**Bournville Cocoa**	1 tablespoon
$\frac{1}{2}$	**lemon**	$\frac{1}{2}$
	yellow food colouring	
about 18	**yellow sugar primroses and daffodils**	about 18
1.2-litre	**ovenproof basin, greased**	2-pint
1	**greaseproof paper piping bag**	1
	small star pipe	

Freeze the cake without the sugar flowers, which will store very well in a dry, clean place.

Making sugar flowers is a good way of using small quantities of left-over royal icing. This is an easy method of decorating cakes at a moment's notice.

Make up the cake mixture as described in the recipe, but do not mix in the cocoa. Divide the mixture into three. Now add the cocoa to one amount, a little essence to a second portion and pink colouring to the third. Spoon the mixtures alternately into the basin, fold through only once to give the cake a marbled effect. Smooth over the top, hollowing out the centre slightly. Bake in a moderate oven (180 c, 350 f, gas 4) for about 1–1¼ hours until well risen and cooked. Test with a skewer to make sure the middle of the cake is cooked. Leave briefly in the basin before turning out to cool on a wire tray.

Have the butter icing made. Blend the cocoa with a spoonful of boiling water then mix into a quarter of the icing. Add the strained lemon juice to the remainder with a little yellow food colouring.

Spread yellow butter icing over the flat side of the cake then cut it in half down the middle. Press the iced surfaces together. Cover the cake with yellow butter icing, spreading it evenly. Lift the cake on to an oval plate. Fit the star pipe into the piping bag and fill the bag with chocolate butter icing. Pipe diagonal lines over the cake in opposite directions so that they cross, making a diamond pattern. Complete the piping with a shell border round the base. Arrange the flowers over the surface, like a traditional chocolate Easter egg.

Serves at least 8

Humpty Dumpty (page 96), Easter Egg Cake and Crispie Nests (page 89)

Humpty Dumpty

(Illustrated on page 95)

Metric		Imperial
	3 egg quantity plain Victoria sponge cake	
	(page 12)	
40 ml	**Bournville Cocoa**	2 tablespoons
350 g	**chocolate butter icing (page 16)**	12 oz
1	**Cadbury's Chocolate Easter Egg**	1
2 squares	**Bournville Dark plain chocolate,**	2 squares
	melted	
	red food colouring	
175 g	**marzipan**	6 oz
18-cm	**square cake tin, greased and base lined,**	7-in
	divided in half with greased, foil-covered card	
7.5-cm	**fluted biscuit cutter**	3-in
	wooden board	

The wall of cake may be frozen.

A divided cake tin, giving two different coloured cakes, makes a more effective wall than using a marbled cake mixture.

To divide the tin, cut a thin piece of card the depth of the cake tin and wrap it in foil. It should be as tight a fit as possible so that no cake mixture seeps through. Grease this foil-covered card as well as the cake tin.

Make up the cake mixture, then divide it in half. Dissolve the cocoa in a little boiling water and mix into one amount. Spread this in half the prepared tin, with the plain mixture in the other half. Bake in a moderately hot oven (190 c, 375 f, gas 5) for about 30 minutes until well risen and cooked. Turn out carefully and cool on a wire tray.

Have the butter icing ready. Slice both cakes horizontally through the middle, then cut all four pieces into four again, widthways across the cake into small rectangles. On a suitable wooden board, build up a wall of cake in alternate colours, making it four layers high. Stick each piece of cake to the other with butter icing and spread a layer on top, reserving just a little butter icing to use later.

Unwrap the egg and paint the rim with melted chocolate, then stick the two halves together. Stand in a jug to set.

Knead red colouring into just over half the marzipan. Roll out the red marzipan about 0.5 cm/$\frac{1}{4}$ in thick and cut out a circle with the biscuit cutter. Place this circle of marzipan in a patty tin or cup and leave it in the refrigerator for about 15 minutes until hard enough to handle. Stand the marzipan cup in the centre of the wall of cake, put a little butter icing in the base then stand the egg in it. Using the red marzipan, cut out two strips for the trousers, a small circle and a round piece for Humpty's hat. Cut two small stars from the scraps of red marzipan to make eyes. Take the plain marzipan and mould thin rolls for arms and legs; a small ball for the nose; a ring for the mouth and two pieces for eyes as shown in the picture. Assemble Humpty Dumpty on the wall. *Serves about 8*

Cute Chicks

(Illustrated on page 99)

(Illustrated on page 99)

The cakes will freeze complete but do not store them too long as small cake items tend to dry out more than larger ones.

The dariole tins are available in different sizes. Make these cakes in the larger ones if possible; although there will be less chicks, they will look more effective.

Press the top of each cake on to a fork so that they are easily held to spread with butter icing. If the icing is not too hard, the crumbly cake mixture will be easier to coat.

Metric		Imperial
125 g	**soft margarine**	4 oz
125 g	**caster sugar**	4 oz
2	**eggs**	2
1	**small orange**	1
125 g	**self-raising flour, sifted**	4 oz
	Decoration	
400 g	**plain butter icing (page 16)**	14 oz
40 ml	**Bournville Cocoa**	2 tablespoons
	yellow food colouring	
125 g	**desiccated coconut**	4 oz
10–14	**sugar orange slices**	10–14
30–40	**silver sugar balls**	30–40
1	**Cadbury's Flake**	1
1 small packet	**Cadbury's Buttons**	1 small packet
15–20	**dariole cake tins, well greased**	15–20
	baking tray	

Cream the margarine and sugar together. Beat in the eggs and the finely grated orange rind. Fold in the flour, then add enough orange juice to make a fairly soft dropping consistency. Three-quarter fill the prepared tins, tapping them on the surface so that the mixture reaches the bottom. Stand on a baking tray and bake in batches according to the number of tins available, in a moderately hot oven (190 c, 375 f, gas 5) for about 25 minutes. Turn out and cool on a wire tray. This mixture will make between 15–20 cakes depending on the actual size of the tins.

Prepare the butter icing according to the recipe instructions. Mix the cocoa with a little boiling water, or hot orange juice and beat it into the icing. Turn the cakes upside down and cover with chocolate icing. Work a few drops of colouring into the coconut, blending it in evenly. Spread on a plate then roll the iced cakes in it.

Cut the orange slices into three triangles. Stick two pieces into each cake, with the points outwards to represent beaks. Press silver balls in for eyes. Cut the Flake into short pieces and use it to make a crest and tail for each of the chick cakes, as shown in the picture. Halve the Buttons and stick them in the sides as flapping wings. *Makes 15–20*

Nest Cake

(Illustrated opposite)

Metric		Imperial
20 ml	**Bournville Cocoa**	1 tablespoon
100 g	**self-raising flour**	$3\frac{1}{2}$ oz
1.25 ml	**salt**	light $\frac{1}{4}$ teaspoon
125 g	**dark soft brown sugar**	4 oz
50 g	**soft margarine**	2 oz
1	**egg**	1
	finely grated rind and juice of $\frac{1}{2}$ orange	
2.5 ml	**vanilla essence**	$\frac{1}{2}$ teaspoon
	Decoration	
100 g	**Bournville Dark plain chocolate**	$3\frac{1}{2}$ oz
50 g	**butter**	2 oz
3	**'Shredded Wheat'**	3
80 ml	**Cadbury's Chocolate Spread**	4 tablespoons
1 large	**Cadbury's Flake**	1 large
125 g	**Cadbury's Mini-Eggs**	4 oz
18-cm/700-ml capacity	**ring mould tin, well greased**	7-in/$1\frac{1}{4}$-pint capacity

Sift the cocoa, flour and salt together into a bowl. Add the sugar, then rub in the margarine. Beat in the egg, finely grated orange rind, strained juice and the essence. Pour this soft batter-type mixture into the prepared tin and bake in a moderate oven (180 c, 350 f, gas 4) for 35–40 minutes until well risen and cooked through. Gently turn out to cool on a wire tray.

Melt the chocolate and butter together in a good sized saucepan. Crumble in the breakfast cereal and stir until it is completely coated in chocolate. Warm the chocolate spread separately, then quickly spread it over the cake and press on the 'Shredded Wheat' mixture. Leave the centre clear but if some mixture remains, put it into the hole once the cake is on a board or plate. Cut the Flake into thin pieces and sprinkle over the top. Leave the chocolate to cool and set before filling the centre with mini-eggs.

The cake may be frozen without the decoration which does not freeze well. Have the chocolate cereal mixture quite hot to press on to a cold cake.

Although rather messy, the easiest way to press on the chocolate cereal mixture is with your fingers; but be careful not to handle it when it is too hot.

The nest is also most effective decorated with thin strips of Flake. Cover the ring cake with 175 g/6 oz chocolate butter icing (page 16), then press on 4 or 5 large Cadbury's Flakes, using the small cut pieces and the crumbs sprinkled over the top. Both cakes may be decorated with the traditional Easter chicks or made at other times of the year. Cadbury's Creme Eggs are generally available all year if the smaller eggs are difficult to find.

Nest Cake, Cute Chicks (page 97) and Bunny Biscuits (page 93)

Cobweb Cake

(Illustrated on page 102)

Metric		Imperial
150 g	**self-raising flour**	5 oz
50 g	**Bournville Cocoa**	2 oz
2.5 ml	**bicarbonate of soda**	½ teaspoon
125 g	**soft margarine**	4 oz
225 g	**dark soft brown sugar**	8 oz
2	**eggs**	2
10 ml	**peppermint essence**	2 teaspoons
25 g	**ground almonds**	1 oz
142 ml	**soured cream**	¼ pint
	Decoration	
50 g	**Bournville Dark plain chocolate**	2 oz
175 g	**icing sugar, sifted**	6 oz
	green food colouring	
1 packet	**Cadbury's Buttons**	1 packet
225 g	**plain butter icing (page 16)**	8 oz
	peppermint essence	
1	**liquorice shoe lace**	1
6	**marshmallows**	6
2 (19-cm)	**round cake tins, greased and base lined**	2 (7½-in)
1	**greaseproof paper piping bag**	1

Freeze the plain cake and decorate when required.

Be careful when adding peppermint flavouring. Peppermint oils are generally much stronger than essences, but it is wise to add any kind of peppermint flavouring slowly.

Warm the chocolate in the piping bag, if it gets too thick. A plain writing pipe may be used but this tends to clog up first and good results can be obtained with just a small hole in the end of the greaseproof paper piping bag.

Icing the cake

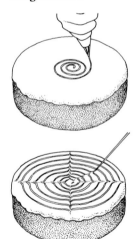

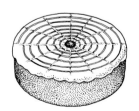

Sift the dry ingredients into a bowl, then add all the other cake ingredients and beat well for about three minutes until thoroughly blended.

Divide the mixture between the tins, hollowing out the centres slightly. Bake in a moderately hot oven (190 c, 375 f, gas 5) for about 35 minutes until well risen and cooked. Turn out and cool on a wire tray.

Melt *half* the chocolate in a small bowl over a pan of hot water. Mix the icing sugar with enough water (or fruit juice) and colouring to make an icing with a fairly thick coating consistency. Put the soft chocolate into the piping bag and cut off the very tip to make a small hole. Spread the icing evenly over one sponge. Immediately pipe a spiral of chocolate from the centre of the cake outwards, as shown in the diagram. Draw twelve straight lines out from the centre with a skewer then place a Button in the centre. Leave to set.

Colour the butter icing green and add essence to taste. Sandwich the cakes together with a little of this butter icing and spread some round the side. Wrap a narrow strip of greaseproof paper round the top half of the side of the cake. Grate the remaining chocolate and press this on to the butter icing below the paper, all round the cake. Take off the paper, carefully easing it away from the butter icing with a knife. Press on a Button below each chocolate line, as shown in the picture. Carefully lift the cake on to a suitable plate or board.

Cut the liquorice into pieces about 2 cm/¾ in long. Press eight pieces into each marshmallow, using a skewer to make holes. Pipe two chocolate eyes and top each with a Button to complete the spiders. Arrange them around the cake.

Serves 10–12

Jumping Jacks

(Illustrated on page 107)

These biscuits freeze well if they are carefully packed to avoid breakages.

Use butter in this recipe as the biscuits tend to spread unevenly if other fat is used – which rather spoils the effect.

The two-colour mixture is particularly attractive. Endeavour to keep the two mixtures from blending together in the piping bag by not adding too much at one time.

Metric		Imperial
175 g	**butter**	6 oz
50 g	**caster sugar**	2 oz
175 g	**plain flour**	6 oz
20 ml	**Bournville Cocoa**	1 tablespoon
	green food colouring	
	peppermint essence	
5	**glacé cherries, quartered**	5
50 g	**Bournville Dark plain chocolate**	2 oz
	large nylon piping bag	
	large star pipe	
	baking tray, greased	

Cream the butter and sugar together really well, until very soft and creamy, then fold in the flour. Halve the mixture and sift the cocoa into one amount, blending it in well. Add a few drops of green colouring and essence to taste to the other portion. Fit the pipe into the bag and fill one side of the bag with the green mixture. Using a spoon, push the chocolate mixture down into the other side of the bag. Pipe four short lines in a close zig-zag on to the prepared baking tray as shown in the picture. Allow room for the biscuits to spread and bake them in batches if necessary. Place a piece of cherry at one end for the taper. Bake in a moderately hot oven (190 c, 375 f, gas 5) for 10–12 minutes until a good colour and cooked. Cool the biscuits on the baking tray for a short while before lifting them on to a wire tray.

Melt the chocolate and either dribble it in lines with a spoon over the biscuits, or fill a greaseproof paper piping bag and pipe lines. Leave to set for a short time. *Makes 18–20*

Halloween Magic

(Illustrated opposite)

Freeze the cake filled and covered in butter icing but without the chocolate decorations.

Children's books are a useful source of inspiration for cake decorations. Trace an outline then prick it on to the cake or pipe it straight on to waxed paper. Chocolate or royal icing decorations will keep for some time in a cool dry place and are handy to have around for an unexpected treat.

Metric		Imperial
50 g	Bournville Dark plain chocolate	2 oz
125 g	butter	4 oz
175 g	soft brown sugar	6 oz
2	eggs, separated	2
175 g	self-raising flour	6 oz
2.5 ml	salt	$\frac{1}{2}$ teaspoon
2.5 ml	ground mixed spice	$\frac{1}{2}$ teaspoon
2.5 ml	ground cinnamon	$\frac{1}{2}$ teaspoon
25 g	chopped candied peel	1 oz
80 ml	milk	4 tablespoons
	Decoration	
80 ml	lemon curd	4 tablespoons
225 g	plain butter icing (page 16)	8 oz
5 ml	ground mixed spice	1 teaspoon
	yellow food colouring	
50 g	Bournville Dark plain chocolate	2 oz
4	Cadbury's Flake from the Family Pack	4
10	chocolate cats (page 104)	10
20-cm	round deep cake tin, greased	8-in
	and base lined	
1	greaseproof paper piping bag	1
	waxed paper	

Melt the chocolate for the cake. Cream the butter and sugar, stir in the egg yolks and melted chocolate. Sift all the dry ingredients together and fold them into the mixture, followed by the peel and milk, mixing well. Whisk the egg whites until stiff and fold them in before turning the mixture into the prepared tin, levelling it carefully. Bake in a warm oven (160 C, 325 F, gas 3) for 1–1$\frac{1}{4}$ hours until well risen and cooked. Turn out and cool on a wire tray.

Slice the cake horizontally through the middle and sandwich it back together with half the lemon curd. Beat the remaining curd into the butter icing with the mixed spice and enough yellow colouring to make a rich colour. Spread this icing all over the cake, making it as smooth as possible.

Trace a suitable witch's outline, first on to a piece of paper and then on the centre of the cake. Melt the chocolate, fill the piping bag with it and cut off just the tip. Follow the marked outline with chocolate, filling in the hair, feet and other suitable features. Pipe star and moon shapes on to the waxed paper, shiny side up, and fill them in with more chocolate. Leave the chocolate to dry completely before peeling the

Cobweb Cake (page 100), Halloween Magic and Shiny Black Hats (page 105)

shapes off the paper and placing them on the cake. Make a broomstick of Flakes and arrange a thin piece on top as the hat brim. Fill in the witch with crumbled Flake.

Lift the cake on to a brightly coloured plate before standing the chocolate cats round the edge. The ones at the back can be made to peep over the top, depending on where the cake is placed on the table. *Serves 10*

Chocolate Cats

(Illustrated on page 102)

Metric		Imperial
100 g	**Bournville Dark plain chocolate**	3½ oz
20–30	**red sugar balls**	20–30
2	**glacé cherries**	2
5	**red liquorice shoe laces**	5
1	**greaseproof paper piping bag**	1
	waxed paper	

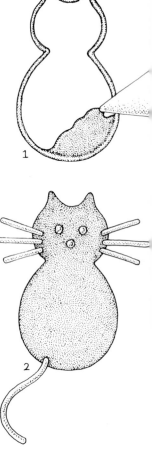

Melt the chocolate carefully in a small bowl over a pan of hot water. Meanwhile, draw or trace one or several cat outlines, each about 6 cm/2¼ in high, on to a piece of white paper. Place waxed paper on top of the drawing, waxed side upwards. Fill the piping bag with melted chocolate, cut off just the tip, then pipe the cat outlines and fill in the centres (1). Make more than you require for the cake in case of breakages. If the chocolate hardens as you are working, put the bag in a warm place to melt the chocolate again.

Press two red eyes in position and cut up small pieces of cherry for noses and liquorice for whiskers and tails (2). Leave the cats to harden for between 1–2 hours, depending on how warm the kitchen is, before carefully peeling them off the paper.

Shiny Black Hats

(Illustrated on page 102 and back cover)

Metric		Imperial
1 packet	**any round Cadbury biscuit**	1 packet
40 ml	**apricot jam**	2 tablespoons
10	**marshmallows**	10
100 g	**Bournville Dark plain chocolate**	3½ oz
5 ml	**bland corn oil**	1 teaspoon
25 g	**caster sugar**	1 oz
40 ml	**water**	2 tablespoons
3	**glacé cherries**	3

Select ten biscuits and spread a little jam on the centre of the plain side of each. Stick a marshmallow on each, with the wide end downwards. Place on a wire tray.

Carefully melt the broken up chocolate, oil, sugar and water together in a small pan over a low heat, stirring until melted and quite smooth. Leave the icing to cool and thicken enough to be able to coat each marshmallow and biscuit completely. Leave the coating to set. Stick a piece of cherry at a jaunty angle on the side of each hat. *Makes 10*

Firework Fountains

(Illustrated on page 107)

Metric		Imperial
250 ml	**condensed milk**	8 fl oz
350 g	**icing sugar, sifted**	12 oz
100 g	**Cadbury's Roast Almond, grated**	3½ oz
	grated rind of ½ lemon	
175 g	**desiccated coconut**	6 oz
50 g	**Bournville Dark plain chocolate**	2 oz
	knob of butter	
2	**glacé cherries**	2

Mix the condensed milk and icing sugar together. Stir in the grated almond chocolate and lemon rind, then work in the coconut until the mixture is pliable. Divide into 15 equal amounts and shape them into pyramids, rolling in between your hands. Stand the pyramids on a tray.

Melt the plain chocolate in a small bowl with the butter. Dip the pointed end of each pyramid into the chocolate and let it run down the sides. Stand a small piece of cherry upright in the top of each cake. Leave to set. *Makes 15*

Catherine Wheel Cake

(Illustrated opposite)

Metric		Imperial
175 g	**soft margarine**	6 oz
175 g	**caster sugar**	6 oz
3	**eggs**	3
175 g	**self-raising flour, sifted**	6 oz
20 ml	**Bournville Cocoa**	1 tablespoon
	pink and green food colouring	
	Decoration	
350 g	**chocolate butter icing (page 16)**	12 oz
175 g	**plain butter icing (page 16), coloured pink**	6 oz
3 (19-cm)	**shallow cake tins, greased and base lined**	3 (7½-in)
2	**greaseproof paper piping bags**	2
	small star pipe	
8	**green or pink cake candles and holders**	8
1	**red cake candle and holder**	1

Freeze the cake complete, wrapping it very carefully. It may be easier to let the icing harden first in the freezer before the cake is wrapped.

The cake can be made in a deep cake tin of the same diameter, with the various colours layered on top of each other. They do run into each other a little, but the cooked cake is still quite effective. Bake for about 55 minutes at the same oven temperature. Cut the cake into three layers, then sandwich together with butter icing.

Cream the margarine and sugar together until pale and light. Beat in the eggs individually, then fold in the flour. Divide the mixture equally into three bowls. Sift the cocoa into one amount, colour another portion pink and add green colouring to the remaining mixture. Spread each colour separately in the prepared cake tins and bake in a moderately hot oven (190 c, 375 f, gas 5) for 20–25 minutes until well risen and cooked. Turn out and cool on a wire tray.

Spread each cake with a little chocolate butter icing and sandwich them together. Reserve equal quantities of both colours of icing, then spread the remaining chocolate icing over the sides of the cake. Run a serrated cake scraper round the side or mark the cake with a fork. Place the pipe in the piping bag, then fill the bag with pink icing. Working from the centre outwards, pipe a spiral scroll of butter icing, leaving space in between as shown in the picture. Empty and discard the bag, clean the pipe, then fill the other bag with chocolate icing and repeat the process, piping a spiral in between the lines of pink icing. Lift the cake on to a suitable plate. Stick the candles in their holders at an angle round the side of the cake with the red one standing straight on the top for the taper. *Serves 10–12*

Bonfire Cake (page 108), Catherine Wheel Cake, Cannon Balls (page 117), Firework Fountains (page 105) and Jumping Jacks (page 101)

Bonfire Cake

(Illustrated on page 107)

Metric		Imperial
1	**pudding basin cake (page 13)**	1
	Decoration	
350 g	**plain butter icing (page 16)**	12 oz
	yellow and red food colouring	
12–16	**Cadbury's Flake from the Family Pack**	12–16
1.2-litre	**ovenproof basin, greased**	2-pint
	guy's head, made from card or marzipan	

Make up and bake the cake as described in the recipe.

Divide the butter icing in half and colour one portion bright yellow and the other a good red. It does not matter if the icing gets a little soft. Spread nice thick lines of alternate colours of butter icing, from the top to the bottom of the turned-out cake, covering it completely. Dip a paint brush into neat food colouring and brush short strokes at irregular intervals over the icing, to highlight the 'flames'. Alternatively, for speed and simplicity, cover the cake completely with just yellow butter icing. Cut the Flakes into thinner strips with a sharp knife. Press the pieces into the icing, letting the brilliant colours show through. Sprinkle the Flake crumbs over the top.

Make the guy's head out of card, drawing on the features, and place it in the centre of the cake. Lift the cake on to a plate or board. *Serves 10–12*

The cake may be wrapped and frozen complete and kept for about a month.

An artistic person could model a head out of marzipan or fondant. It needs to be about 5 cm/2 in high, with a black paper or marzipan hat on top. A whole small Flake may be pushed in behind the guy to represent the stake.

Individual Ideas

Small children love small cakes and when you make the delicious examples from this chapter you will find that adults love them, too! Cupid Biscuits, Praline Swirls and Scottish Fingers are favourites of children and adults alike, while Frosty Bears or Clowns will bring a smile to every child's face.

Sausage Dogs

(Illustrated on page 23)

Freeze complete for up to a month, standing them in a firm container so that they do not break or become squashed.

As the cooking time is short, the whisked sponge mixture should stay firm enough for it to be cooked in batches if enough sponge finger tins are not available to cook it all at once. Make an even number.

Metric		Imperial
2	**eggs, size 2**	2
50 g	**caster sugar**	2 oz
50 g	**plain flour**	2 oz
15 ml	**Bournville Cocoa**	3 teaspoons
5	**glacé cherries**	5
20	**currants**	20
1	**Cadbury's Flake, crumbled**	1
142 ml	**double cream**	$\frac{1}{4}$ pint
10	**short strips angelica**	10

tray of sponge finger tins, greased and floured
nylon piping bag
medium star pipe

Whisk the eggs and sugar with an electric mixer or in a bowl over hot water, for about 10 minutes until the whisk leaves a definite trail in the mixture. Fold in the flour and cocoa, sifted together, being careful not to knock out the air but leaving no pockets of flour in the mixture. Spoon the mixture neatly into each tin. Place half a cherry at one end for a nose and two currants just behind for eyes, on only half the total number of cakes. Bake in a fairly hot oven (200 C, 400 F, gas 6) for 10–12 minutes until firm and springy to the touch. Turn out to cool on a wire tray. Bake another batch in the same way, making about 20 sponge fingers in all. Sprinkle the crumbled Flake along the top of the decorated sponges whilst they are still hot. Leave to cool completely.

The mixture can also be piped on to well greased and floured baking trays, with a 2-cm/¾-in plain nozzle. Make them the same length by marking straight lines at least 7.5 cm/3 in long on the trays, spacing them well apart.

Whisk the cream until it will hold its shape. Fit the pipe into the piping bag and fill with the cream. Pipe quite a thick layer of cream on the underside of the plain sponges, then sandwich a decorated and plain sponge finger together. Put a star of cream at the tail end of each and stand a small piece of angelica in it. *Makes about 10*

Frosty Bears

(Illustrated opposite and on back cover)

Metric		Imperial
50 g	**soft margarine**	2 oz
50 g	**soft brown sugar**	2 oz
2	**eggs**	2
50 g	**self-raising flour**	2 oz
40 ml	**Bournville Cocoa**	2 tablespoons
125 g	**soft cream cheese**	4 oz
25 g	**caster sugar**	1 oz
	Decoration	
1.5 litres	**vanilla ice cream**	2½ pints
1 packet	**Cadbury's Buttons**	1 packet
14 g	**seedless raisins**	½ oz
1	**liquorice shoe lace**	1
12	**paper cake cases**	12
	baking tray	

The cakes can be packed and frozen separately, ready to use later or complete the bears and freeze them in a rigid container for about a week.

To speed assembly, scoop out the ice cream on to a baking tray and leave in the freezer until required.

Beat the margarine, brown sugar, 1 egg, flour and cocoa together in a bowl for about 2 minutes until well mixed and smooth. Divide the mixture equally between the cake cases. Beat the cream cheese to soften, then add the caster sugar and remaining egg. Drop a good teaspoonful of the cheese mixture on to each little cake. Arrange them fairly close together on the baking tray and bake in a moderate oven (180 C, 350 F, gas 4) for about 30 minutes until well risen and cooked. Cool the cakes in their cases on a wire tray.

Just before they are required, place a good scoopful of ice cream on each little cake, pressing it on quite firmly. Press two Buttons into the top of each one for ears, three raisins for the eyes and nose and a small piece of liquorice for the mouth. Complete all of them in the same way and serve immediately. *Makes 12*

Frosty Bears, Sunbathing Penguins (page 29) and Frogland (page 21)

Cupid Biscuits

(Illustrated on page 63)

Metric		Imperial
50 g	**plain flour**	2 oz
50 g	**ground almonds**	2 oz
50 g	**butter**	2 oz
40 ml	**caster sugar**	2 tablespoons
40 ml	**Cadbury's Drinking Chocolate**	2 tablespoons
1	**egg yolk**	1
	Icing	
225 g	**sugar, sifted**	8 oz
	lemon juice	
	pink food colouring	
4	**Cadbury's Flake from the Family Pack**	4
50 g	**Bournville Dark plain chocolate**	2 oz
	heart-shaped biscuit cutter	
	baking tray, greased	
1	**greaseproof paper piping bag**	1

As these biscuits are quite sweet, use a sharp fruit juice, not water, to make up the icing. They look effective and children also like to see their initials on their own biscuit. Store in an airtight container when the icing is absolutely dry.

Halve Cadbury's Flake by cutting it down the middle lengthways, with a sharp knife, in one definite movement. It should not flake up. A whole Flake looks too heavy on these biscuits.

If a heart-shaped cutter is not available, trace a suitable sized heart shape on to clean cardboard and cut it out. Use this shape to cut out the biscuits.

Mix the flour and ground almonds together, then rub in the butter. Add the sugar and drinking chocolate and bind the mixture together with the egg yolk. Roll out on a lightly floured surface to about 0.5 cm/$\frac{1}{4}$ in thick and cut out heart-shaped biscuits. Knead and roll the biscuit dough in between. Arrange on the prepared baking tray and bake in a moderate oven (180 C, 350 F, gas 4) for about 12 minutes. Leave to harden slightly before lifting off the baking tray.

Make up a fairly thick coating icing with the icing sugar and lemon juice, adding colouring to make a pretty pink. Carefully ice each biscuit, letting the icing flow smoothly over the edges. Lift them on to a wire tray. Cut the Flake straight down the middle and lay one piece diagonally across each biscuit, before the icing has set. Leave to harden.

Melt the chocolate, then pour into the piping bag. Cut off the tip and pipe chocolate initials on each biscuit. *Makes 8*

Clown Cakes

(Illustrated on page 114)

These could be used as place names at a party, with gaily coloured cards, particularly if a suitable theme is chosen.

Metric		Imperial
	Hats	
50 g	**Bournville Dark plain chocolate**	2 oz
	knob of butter	
40 ml	**water**	2 tablespoons
25 g	**icing sugar**	1 oz
4	**wafer ice cream cones**	4
1 large packet	**Cadbury's Buttons**	1 large packet
	Base	
4	**chocolate buns (page 16)**	4
175 g	**chocolate butter icing (page 16)**	6 oz
1 large packet	**Cadbury's Buttons**	1 large packet
	Heads	
75 g	**chocolate cake crumbs**	3 oz
75 g	**ground almonds**	3 oz
20 ml	**orange juice or sherry**	1 tablespoon
30 ml	**apricot jam, heated**	1 good tablespoon
40 ml	**icing sugar, sifted**	2 tablespoons
50 g	**plain butter icing (page 16)**	2 oz
12	**silver sugar balls**	12
2	**glacé cherries, halved**	2
4	**deep Yorkshire pudding tins**	4
4	**decorative paper cake cases**	4
	greaseproof paper piping bag	
	star pipe	

Melt the chocolate, butter and water together in a pan. Sift the icing sugar into a small, deep bowl, then beat in the chocolate mixture until smooth. Dip the cones into the chocolate, using a pastry brush to completely cover them. Place six Buttons round each base and set on waxed paper.

Make the chocolate buns according to the recipe instructions. Cover each up turned cake with the butter icing, cut the Buttons in half and arrange them round the cake bases, then lift carefully on to small up turned saucers.

Work the cake crumbs, ground almonds, orange juice or sherry and jam together, divide into four and roll into balls. Use icing sugar to prevent the mixture sticking to your hands. Stand a paper case on each base, with the pattern upwards as shown in the picture and place a ball shape on top. Press a hat on to each. Fit the star pipe into the piping bag and fill with butter icing. Pipe a ruff round the neck of each cake, two eyes on each face and a pom-pom on the hats. Press silver balls on the eyes and hats. Add a cherry nose. *Makes 4*

Pantomime Mice

(Illustrated opposite and on front cover)

The frosting is easiest to make with an electric hand mixer and will probably take between 8–10 minutes. It is worth timing the whisking the first time you make the frosting, as it is quite difficult to know when it is whisked enough. If too soft, it will not harden on the outside and retain its shape. Work as quickly as possible once the frosting is whisked to retain the glossy appearance.

Using a small palette (flat-bladed) knife helps avoid cake crumbs mixing with the frosting. Keep the knife level on the surface of the frosting as much as possible.

Heat the chocolate spread a little if it is difficult to spread.

Metric		Imperial
125 g	**plain flour**	4 oz
25 g	**Bournville Cocoa**	1 oz
10 ml	**baking powder**	2 teaspoons
25 g	**ground almonds**	1 oz
150 g	**caster sugar**	5 oz
2	**eggs, separated**	2
100 ml	**milk**	5 tablespoons
120 ml	**bland salad oil**	6 tablespoons
2.5 ml	**vanilla essence**	$\frac{1}{2}$ teaspoon
60 ml	**Cadbury's Chocolate Spread**	3 tablespoons
	Icing	
2	**egg whites, size 2**	2
350 g	**icing sugar, sifted**	12 oz
1.25 ml	**cream of tartar**	$\frac{1}{4}$ teaspoon
pinch of	**salt**	pinch of
80 ml	**water**	4 tablespoons
	Decoration	
	red food colouring	
75 g	**marzipan**	3 oz
1 small packet	**Cadbury's Buttons**	1 small packet
16	**red sugar balls**	16
1	**glacé cherry**	1
2	**thin liquorice shoe laces**	2
1.2-litre	**ovenproof basin, well greased**	2-pint
2.5-cm	**round pastry cutter**	1-in

Sift the flour, cocoa and baking powder into a bowl. Add the almonds and sugar. Mix in the egg yolks, milk, oil and essence until quite smooth. Whisk the egg whites fairly stiffly and fold in carefully, then pour the soft mixture into the greased bowl. Bake in a moderate oven (180 c, 350 f, gas 4) for about 55 minutes until well risen and cooked through. Test with a skewer before turning out. Immediately slice the cake in half horizontally and sandwich together again with chocolate spread. Leave to cool before cutting into 8 wedges.

Measure all the icing ingredients into a fairly large bowl and stand this over a pan of hot water. Whisk hard until the frosting is glossy, white and smooth, standing in stiff peaks. Spread the frosting over the triangular pieces 'of cake, covering them liberally and leaving the surface in peaks. Keep the bowl of frosting over the hot water while you cover the cakes.

Work a little colouring evenly into the marzipan then roll

Pantomime Mice, Circus Ring (page 69) and Clown Cakes (page 113).

out and cut out 16 circles with the cutter. Pinch one side of the circles to form ears and stand two ears in the icing on the top of each cake as shown in the picture. Stick a sugar ball on to the centre of each Button with a little icing and place these eyes on each cake. Cut the cherry into eight triangles and place one piece as a nose on each cake with small pieces of liquorice for the whiskers. Stick a longer piece of liquorice in to form a tail. Allow the icing to harden for a couple of hours. *Makes 8*

Loot Biscuits

(Illustrated on page 78)

Metric		Imperial
175 g	**plain flour**	6 oz
50 g	**rice flour**	2 oz
50 g	**caster sugar**	2 oz
125 g	**butter**	4 oz
10 ml	**lemon juice**	2 teaspoons
	yellow and green food colouring	
a few drops	**almond essence**	a few drops
5 ml	**milk**	1 teaspoon
	a little icing sugar, sifted	
	Decoration	
225 g	**royal icing (page 17)**	8 oz
3 small packets	**Cadbury's Buttons**	3 small packets
75 g	**glacé cherries**	3 oz
	tree and star-shaped biscuit cutters	
2	**baking trays, well greased**	2
1	**greaseproof paper piping bag**	1
	plain writing pipe	

The biscuits will keep quite well if stored in an airtight container, but they will go soft if left in the open air too long.

Children might well enjoy creating their own designs on the biscuits. The decoration can easily be altered to fit into the theme of a party.

Mix the flours and sugar together and rub in the butter until the mixture resembles fine breadcrumbs. Divide the mixture in half, adding lemon juice and a little yellow colouring to one amount and the green colouring, essence and milk to the other portion. Knead both mixtures separately, then roll out the biscuit doughs in turn on a lightly sugared surface. Cut out yellow stars and green trees, making about 18 of each. Bake the biscuits on the prepared baking trays in a moderate oven (180 C, 350 F, gas 4) for 10–15 minutes until cooked. Lift off and cool on a wire tray.

Cut the tip off the piping bag and drop in the pipe. Fill with royal icing and pipe a variety of designs on the biscuits, using the Buttons and cherries as decoration, as shown in the picture. Leave to dry. *Makes about 36*

Artillery Cannons

(Illustrated on page 75)

(Illustrated on page 75)

❋

The Swiss roll will freeze but it is better to assemble the cakes as required.

Metric		Imperial
1	**chocolate Swiss roll, filled (page 14)**	1
50 g	**butter**	2 oz
75 g	**icing sugar, sifted**	3 oz
	vanilla essence	
4 large	**Cadbury's Flakes**	4 large
50 g	**aniseed balls**	2 oz
	small star pipe	
1	**greaseproof paper piping bag**	1

Prepare and fill the Swiss roll as described in the recipe. Cream the butter with the icing sugar and a few drops of essence until soft and pale. Fit the star pipe into the piping bag and fill with the butter icing. Cut the Swiss roll into twelve even slices, then cut four slices in half. Place two halves together side by side, flat sides down and press two whole slices on either side. Pipe a zig-zag of icing down the middle and rest a Flake on it at an angle as shown in the picture. Make all the cannons in the same way. Pile up the aniseed balls beside the cannons and arrange toy soldiers round about if available. *Makes 4*

Cannon Balls

(Illustrated on page 107)

(Illustrated on page 107)

This is another recipe that older children can make. These cannon balls are very tempting so try to see that all the delicious, sticky mixture goes round the marshmallows.

Metric		Imperial
40 g	**butter or hard margarine**	1½ oz
40 ml	**Bournville Cocoa**	2 tablespoons
60 ml	**condensed milk**	3 tablespoons
50 g	**light soft brown sugar**	2 oz
150 g	**desiccated coconut**	5 oz
125 g	**marshmallows**	4 oz

Melt the butter or margarine, cocoa, condensed milk and sugar together, in a saucepan, stirring continuously. Reserve 25 g/1 oz of the coconut before stirring the remaining coconut into the melted mixture, with the pan off the heat. When the mixture is cool enough to handle, divide it into 12 equal amounts. Flatten the rather sticky mixture between the palms of your hands, then mould this round a marshmallow and roll into a ball. Make them all in the same way before tossing in the reserved coconut, pressing it on slightly. Leave to harden a little before eating. *Makes 12*

Scottish Fingers

(Illustrated opposite)

Metric		Imperial
175 g	**butter**	6 oz
75 g	**caster sugar**	3 oz
175 g	**plain flour**	6 oz
75 g	**cornflour**	3 oz
	grated rind of 1 orange	
25 g	**chopped nuts, for example walnuts,**	1 oz
	hazelnuts or peanuts	
25 g	**seedless raisins**	1 oz
	Topping	
125 g	**butter or margarine**	4 oz
125 ml	**condensed milk**	scant $\frac{1}{4}$ pint
125 g	**caster sugar**	4 oz
40 ml	**golden syrup**	2 tablespoons
1	**Cadbury's Flake Family Pack**	1
28 × 18-cm	**Swiss roll tin**	11 × 7-in

Should the caramel be ready before the base is cooked, stand the pan in cold water to prevent it cooking any further. It is most important to cook the caramel correctly.

This is a recipe that would be particularly popular at fund raising events. Cut the fingers in half with a sharp knife to make them go further.

Cream the butter and sugar together thoroughly for the shortbread base. Sift together the flours and add them to the creamed mixture with the finely grated orange rind, nuts and fruit, mixing well. If the mixture becomes sticky, sprinkle in a little extra flour. Press into the tin and level the surface with a knife before pricking all over with a fork. Bake in a warm oven (160 c, 325 f, gas 3) for 25–30 minutes until golden brown. Leave in the tin.

Meanwhile prepare the topping by dissolving all the ingredients except the Flakes in a saucepan over a low heat, stirring occasionally. When the sugar grains have disappeared completely and the mixture is smooth, bring to the boil and continue cooking carefully for 5 minutes, stirring continuously so the base does not burn. When it is a nice rich colour, pour over the shortbread base in the tin. Cut into 18 even-sized fingers and place a Flake on each whilst the caramel is still quite hot. Leave to cool before lifting the fingers out of the tin. Store in an airtight container.

Makes 18

Braemar Men (page 120), Scottish Fingers and Loch Ness Monster (page 80)

Praline Swirls

(Illustrated on page 66)

Metric		Imperial
100 g	**Bournville Dark plain chocolate**	3½ oz
50 g	**butter**	2 oz
1.25 ml	**vanilla essence**	¼ teaspoon
75 g	**icing sugar, sifted**	3 oz
25 g	**hazelnuts, finely ground**	1 oz
18	**crystallised violets**	18
18	**paper sweet cases**	18
	nylon piping bag	
	medium star pipe	

For a special occasion, stir in a spoonful of brandy, rum or liqueur.

Break up the chocolate and melt it, with the butter, in a pan over a low heat. Off the heat, stir in the essence, then the icing sugar and hazelnuts. Beat well to thoroughly mix. Fill the piping bag with this mixture, then pipe a good whirl into each of the cases placed on a tray. Place a violet on each and leave to firm up in the refrigerator for at least 30 minutes.

Makes 18

Braemar Men

(Illustrated on the title spread and page 119)

Metric		Imperial
175 g	**plain flour**	6 oz
pinch of	**salt**	pinch of
125 g	**butter**	4 oz
50 g	**caster sugar**	2 oz
	Decoration	
50 g	**icing sugar, sifted**	2 oz
1 metre	**tartan ribbon**	39 in
6	**Cadbury's Buttons**	6
12	**currants**	12
2	**glacé cherries**	2
6	**Cadbury's Flakes**	6
	gingerbread man cutter	
	baking tray, lightly floured	
1	**greaseproof paper piping bag**	1

Do not roll the shortbread too thin or the biscuits tend to break. The quantity of mixture is exactly right to make six biscuits. Either size of Flake may be used: the larger size looks more correct but the smaller Flakes are not so heavy on the biscuits.

Should you only have a gingerbread woman cutter, make a sharp cut through the skirt with a knife and divide the legs.

Sift the flour and salt together. Rub in the butter until the mixture resembles breadcrumbs, then add the sugar. Knead the mixture into a pliable dough. Roll out on a lightly floured surface to just under 1 cm/$\frac{1}{4}$ in thick. Cut out the shapes with the cutter, rolling the excess dough again in between, making six in all. Move one arm of each man closer to his side. Bake on the prepared baking tray in a warm oven (160 C, 325 F, gas 3) for about 30 minutes until pale brown. Cool before lifting off the tray.

Blend the icing sugar with just enough water or fruit juice to make a thick glacé icing and fill the piping bag. Cut the ribbon into six even lengths. Cut the tip off the bag and secure the ribbon over the shoulder of each man, sticking the ends at the back with icing. Use a little icing to stick a Button in position on the heads, two currants for eyes and a piece of cherry for a cheerful mouth. Finally add a Flake 'caber' (see picture). Allow the icing to dry. *Makes 6*

Sleepers

(Illustrated on page 38)

Inaccurately measured syrup can mean that the recipe will not work. Always measure syrup with a hot, metal tablespoon, holding the spoon with an oven cloth. If the syrup is very thick in the tin, pop it into a warm oven for a short time to melt so that it is easier to spoon out.

Metric		Imperial
50 g	**Bournville Dark plain chocolate**	2 oz
75 g	**butter**	3 oz
60 ml	**golden syrup**	3 tablespoons
75 g	**sugar**	3 oz
225 g	**rolled oats**	8 oz
pinch of	**salt**	pinch of
50 g	**sultanas**	2 oz
	Icing	
100 g	**Bournville Dark plain chocolate**	3½ oz
10 ml	**bland salad oil**	2 teaspoons
60 ml	**water**	3 tablespoons
50 g	**butter**	2 oz
18 × 28-cm	**shallow tin, greased**	7 × 11-in

Break the chocolate into a pan and melt it with the butter, syrup and sugar without boiling. Off the heat, stir in the oats, salt and sultanas to make a flapjack mixture, then press the mixture evenly into the prepared tin. Bake in a moderate oven (180 C, 350 F, gas 4) for 20–25 minutes. Whilst still hot, cut the flapjack lengthways down the middle and then into 1.25-cm/ $\frac{1}{2}$-in wide pieces, making 24 pieces in all. Leave to cool completely before lifting out of the tin.

Melt all the icing ingredients together in a small bowl over a pan of hot water. Dip both ends of the flapjack pieces into the icing and leave to dry on a wire tray. *Makes 24*

Trefoil Biscuits

(Illustrated on title spread and opposite)

Metric		Imperial
150 g	**soft brown sugar**	5 oz
50 g	**Cadbury's Drinking Chocolate**	2 oz
1	**egg**	1
200 g	**self-raising flour, sifted**	7 oz
	finely grated rind of 2 lemons	
75 g	**butter, melted**	3 oz
	Icing	
450 g	**icing sugar, sifted**	1 lb
	juice of 2 lemons	
	yellow food colouring	
2 large packets	**Cadbury's Buttons**	2 large packets
	baking tray, greased	
1	**greaseproof paper piping bag**	1

The undecorated biscuits freeze well.

Polish the Buttons by resting them in the palm of your hand and rubbing them lightly with your finger. This will remove any loose chocolate from the surface of the Buttons and bring them up to a nice shine.

Measure the sugar and drinking chocolate into a bowl, then stir in the egg. Add the flour and lemon rind. Bind to a stiff dough with the butter. Divide the mixture into three even amounts, then roll each one into a sausage shape no more than 2.5 cm/1 in wide – make all three the same length. Wrap separately in greaseproof paper and chill for about 30 minutes.

Cut each roll into thin slices about 0.5 cm/$\frac{1}{4}$ in thick. Overlap three circles on the baking tray, making a trefoil shape. Continue until most of the mixture is used. Roll out a small piece and chop into stalk sized pieces to stick on each biscuit. Bake in a moderate oven (180 c, 350 f, gas 4) for 10–12 minutes. Lift off and cool on a wire tray.

Make a thick coating icing with the icing sugar and strained lemon juice, adding enough food colouring to make a good rich gold colour. Place a good spoonful of the icing in the piping bag. Add a little more liquid to the remaining icing to make it a little thinner. Decorate the biscuits about six at a time, by piping a border of icing round the edge of each biscuit, then filling in the centre with the softer icing. Overlap three Buttons in the centre of each biscuit. Make all the biscuits in the same way and leave to dry. *Makes about 30*

Tracking Cake (page 48), Patrol Tents (page 124) and Trefoil biscuits

Patrol Tents

(Illustrated on page 123)

Metric		Imperial
25 g	**Bournville Cocoa**	1 oz
125 g	**self-raising flour**	4 oz
2	**eggs**	2
125 g	**soft margarine**	4 oz
125 g	**caster sugar**	4 oz
	Decoration	
100 ml	**red jam**	5 tablespoons
150 ml	**desiccated coconut**	4 heaped tablespoons
125 g	**chocolate butter icing (page 16)**	4 oz
2 packets	**Cadbury's Fingers**	2 packets
9	**dariole moulds, well greased**	9
	baking tray	
	small star pipe	
	greaseproof paper piping bag	
9	**paper cake cases**	9
	patrol badges and flags	

Sift the cocoa and flour into a bowl, then add the remaining cake ingredients. Beat really well, making the cake by the one-stage method. Half fill the prepared tins with mixture, stand them on the baking tray and bake in a moderately hot oven (190 c, 375 f, gas 5) for about 25 minutes until well risen and cooked right through. Shake out on to a wire tray to cool.

Melt the jam with two spoonfuls of water. Brush the cakes with jam and roll them in the coconut spread on a plate. Fit the pipe into the piping bag and fill with chocolate butter icing. Pipe a good whirl on the top of each cake. Stand them on the flattened paper cases and lean five or six Finger biscuits against each cake, to make tents. Allocate tents to a 'patrol' with a badge as shown in the picture and stick flags in some cakes. *Makes 9*

The cakes, coated with jam and coconut may be frozen. Pack in a rigid container and keep for about a month. Complete the decoration as required.

Tap the tins, filled with the uncooked cake mixture, on the work surface so that no pockets of air are left and the cakes bake evenly.

The easiest way to spread these small castle cakes with jam is to push them on to a short skewer, brush with jam then roll in the coconut.

Lollipop Biscuits

(Illustrated on page 126)

Small wooden sticks, but not cocktail sticks, or even clean ice lolly sticks are ideal for these biscuits. Avoid plastic sticks as they will melt in the oven.

To make the biscuits stay on the sticks, push them right in but do not allow the stick to show through the mixture. The baked biscuit will then harden and stay on the stick to be held upright.

Metric		Imperial
	Plain shortbread	
175 g	**plain flour**	6 oz
125 g	**butter**	4 oz
50 g	**caster sugar**	2 oz
	finely grated rind and juice of $\frac{1}{2}$ lemon	
	Chocolate shortbread	
125 g	**plain flour**	4 oz
75 g	**butter**	3 oz
10 ml	**Bournville Cocoa, sifted**	2 teaspoons
50 g	**caster sugar**	2 oz
	vanilla essence	
	a little icing sugar, sifted	
	Decoration	
20 ml	**apricot jam**	1 tablespoon
20 ml	**coloured sugar strands**	1 tablespoon
20	**lollipop sticks**	20
2	**baking trays, greased**	2

Prepare the plain shortbread first. Sift the flour into a bowl and rub in the butter until the mixture resembles fine breadcrumbs. Add the sugar, lemon rind and the strained juice and bind into a firm dough. Chill this dough whilst making the chocolate shortbread in the same way, adding the cocoa, sugar and essence to the rubbed-in ingredients.

Dust the surface lightly with icing sugar. Roll each piece of dough separately into rectangles measuring about 20 × 30 cm/8 × 12 in. Lift the chocolate dough on top of the plain mixture and roll up from the narrow end, like a Swiss roll. Cut into 20 even slices and place slightly apart on baking trays. Press a lollipop stick into each biscuit. Bake in a moderately hot oven (190 c, 375 f, gas 5) for about 20 minutes until golden brown. Leave the biscuits on the baking tray to harden before finally cooling them on a wire tray.

Spread a little jam in the centre of each biscuit and sprinkle with sugar strands. Store in an airtight container. *Makes 20*

Index